"When it comes to holocausts or other horrors, most of us assume God has his hands tied and his back to the wall. We figure the devil wreaks havoc when God's not looking; we rationalize the Lord's 'mistakes,' figuring he absentmindedly took his hands off the wheel when tragedies happen. But John Piper paints a different picture from the pages of Scripture that will strengthen your heart, bolster your faith, and deepen your understanding of the 'largeness' of God's sovereignty."
> —JONI EARECKSON TADA, Joni and Friends International
> Disability Center

"I had to read this book twice. The weighty truths about the sovereign wisdom and power of God unpacked in these pages created in me an overwhelming feeling of gratitude and ultimate safety. To be reminded of his might over everything is priceless, and I don't think I'll ever be able to preach the same again."
> —MATT CHANDLER, Lead Pastor, The Village Church,
> Highland Village, Texas

"Pastors, make sure your people read this book! I know of no one who has so clearly addressed the relationship of man's sin and God's sovereignty as John has done in *Spectacular Sins*."
> —RANDY POPE, Pastor, Perimeter Church, Duluth, GA

"*Spectacular Sins and Their Global Purpose in the Glory of Christ*. Wow! *Spectacular* and *sin*! I've never seen those words together before. And who but John Piper could so brilliantly weave them into the same lyric as the global, purposeful glory of Christ! This man never ceases to inspire me to be more awestruck with the supremacy of Jesus."
> —CHRIS TOMLIN, song-writer and lead worshiper

"'Wimpy worldviews make wimpy Christians'—this is the repeated refrain in these pages. But there is nothing wimpy about the worldview provided in *Spectacular Sins*. It dares to ask—and answer—the most daunting question for the Christian: '*Why* do sin, suffering, and evil exist in a world where God is sovereign?' Dr. Piper has provided an honest, biblical, and pastoral theodicy for our generation. These pages turn the lights on in the darkest room of Christian theology."
> —RICK HOLLAND, Executive pastor, Grace Community Church
> and Director of the Resolved Conference

"It is impossible to truly apprehend the magnificent comfort of God's sovereignty before we first consider that sovereignty in light of pain, suffering, evil, and sin. In this little book, John Piper is sending the church a precious gift by demonstrating how the fallenness of this world has been designed for our ultimate good and God's ultimate glory. It is a biblical, impassioned plea for this generation to consider God's world in light of God's word. He who has an ear, let him hear!"

  —MILES V. VAN PELT, Reformed Theological Seminary,
    Jackson, Mississippi

"I wish I could have read this book as a new Christian as I was unprepared to face calamity because of my deficient view of God's sovereignty. I am delighted now as a young pastor to be able to hand my congregation this book that will enable them to see and worship God in their suffering."

  —DARRIN PATRICK, Pastor of The Journey, St. Louis

"Don't let the small size of this book fool you. Like most of Piper's writings, it's wonderfully dangerous and critically needed in our day—especially in the Western world. This is a stick of gospel dynamite that has the potential of radically altering the way you view suffering and evil forever—on both a personal and global scale. But I must warn you. Don't expect to find in this book all the typical, soft 'words of comfort' espoused by many in our day to help people maximize pleasure by minimizing or rationalizing away the pain of suffering. Instead prepare yourself to have your mind renewed by the deep, weighty truths of God's word, your faith strengthened by a renewed vision of God's supremacy in all things (including evil), and your courage bolstered in the face of the inevitable suffering that lies ahead to follow hard by faith after the One whose death was the most spectacular sin—for the sake of the nations and the glory of God. Only this can bring you the true comfort of God in the face of suffering and evil. I highly recommend it!"

  —STEVEN L. CHILDERS, President & CEO, Global Church
    Advancement; Associate Professor of Practical Theology,
    Reformed Theological Seminary, Orlando, Florida

SPECTACULAR SINS

BOOKS BY JOHN PIPER

JOHN PIPER

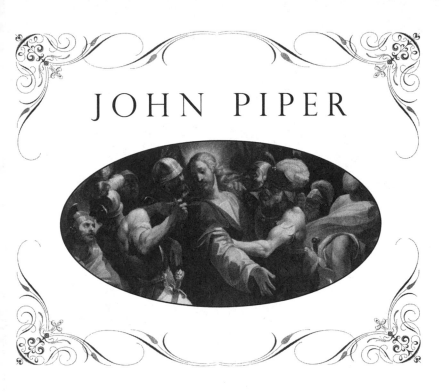

SPECTACULAR
SINS

AND THEIR GLOBAL PURPOSE
IN THE GLORY OF CHRIST

CROSSWAY BOOKS
WHEATON, ILLINOIS

PDF ISBN: 978-1-4335-0474-7

Mobipocket ISBN: 978-1-4335-0475-4

Library of Congress Cataloging-in-Publication Data
Piper, John, 1946–
   Spectacular sins : and their global purpose in the glory of Christ /
John Piper.
     p. cm.
   Includes bibliographical references and index.
   ISBN 978-1-4335-0275-0 (hc)
   1. Sin—Biblical teaching. 2. Sin—Christianity. I. Title.
BS680.S57P57   2008
241'.3—dc22
                            2008010514

LB		18	17	16	15	14	13	12	11	10	09	08
15	14	13	12	11	10	9	8	7	6	5	4	3	2	1

To Joseph
whose life of suffering and salvation said,
"You meant evil against me,
but God meant it for good."

CONTENTS

INTRODUCTION:
THE TIMES ARE CHANGING

When the Bruised Heart Needs a Tire Iron

Jesus Christ, who was in the beginning with God, and *was* God (John 1:1), created the universe. He did this as God the Father's equal and as his agent. "All things were made *through* him" (John 1:3; 1 Cor. 8:6; Heb. 1:2). And he did it to display his glory. "*By* him all things were created . . . and *for* him" (Col. 1:16). *By* him and *for* him. All things were created by Christ and for Christ. The Son of God, who has become a human being—the God-man, Jesus of Nazareth—in perfect concert with his Father, created the universe for the display of his all-satisfying glory.

Not only that, he holds it all together with total authority. "He is the radiance of the glory of God and the exact imprint of his nature, and he upholds the universe by the word of his power" (Heb. 1:3). How this massive power—to create and uphold the universe—is wielded to display the glory of Christ is the great issue of our time, and of all time.

THE GREATEST DISPLAY OF THE GLORY OF CHRIST

The apex of the glory of Christ is the glory of his grace—treating people infinitely better than they deserve—giving himself for the everlasting joy of the worst of sinners who will have him as their highest Treasure. And the apex of this grace is the murder of the God-man outside Jerusalem around A.D. 33. The death of Jesus Christ was murder. It was the most spectacular sin ever committed.

At the all-important pivot of human history, the worst sin ever committed served to show the greatest glory of Christ and obtain the sin-conquering gift of God's grace. God did not just overcome evil at the cross. He made evil serve the overcoming of evil. He made evil commit suicide in doing its worst evil.

Evil is anything and everything opposed to the fullest display of the glory of Christ. That's the meaning of evil. In the death of Christ, the powers of darkness did their best to destroy the glory of the Son of God. This is the apex of evil. But instead they found themselves quoting the script of ancient prophecy and acting the part assigned by God. Precisely in putting Christ to death, they put his glory on display—the very glory that they aimed to destroy. The apex of evil achieved the apex of the glory of Christ. The glory of grace.

TO SEE THE WORLD DIFFERENTLY

When you see this, and feel the force of it, the way you look at the world changes. I am writing this book because I think the days that are coming will demand from the followers of Christ this change in the way we look at the world. It seems to me that Christians in the West are being coddled. We suffer little in the name of Christ. Therefore, we read the Bible not with a desperate hunger for evidences of God's triumph in pain, but with a view to improving our private pleasures.

Therefore, we read the Bible selectively. We pick a text here and there to fit our felt needs. This is like a doctor who forgets how to write prescriptions for the best antibiotics because everybody seems healthy, and he has spent the last decades tweaking good health with hip-hop exercise videos, unaware that pestilence is at the door. It's like the soldier who forgets how to use his weapons because the times seem peaceful, and he has spent the last decades doing relief work and teaching the children how to play games.

THE TIMES ARE CHANGING

But the times are changing. For seventy million baby boomers, for example, life has changed. It seems very short now. What used to be a fond nostalgia for the sixties has turned into an ache that the beloved decade is now so far away that its main meaning is: we are dying. Different ages get the message in different ways.

And not only life, but the world too is shrinking. People who don't like Christians are all around us. Only a strange providence keeps our churches from being bombed. It is only a matter of time till the reality of the rest of the world comes home. And all the while we are called by Christ to go to *them*, love them, sacrifice for them, bring the gospel to them. The Great Commission is not child's play. It is costly. Very costly.

The coddled Western world will sooner or later give way to great affliction. And when it does, whose vision of God will hold? Where are Christians being prepared for great global sorrows? Where is the Christian mind and soul being prepared for the horrors to come? Christians in the West are weakened by wimpy worldviews. And wimpy worldviews make wimpy Christians. God is weightless in our lives. He is not terrifyingly magnificent. His sovereignty is secondary (at best) to his sensitivity.

THE MISSING BIBLE

What is missing is the Bible. I mean the whole Bible, with its blood and guts and sins and horrors—and all of it under the massive hand of God. The hand whose fingers flick stars into being. The hand that gives life and takes it. The hand that rules everything. Everything. What we need is to know the great things about God. Knowing great things about God will help make us ready not to collapse under cataclysmic conflict and personal catastrophe.

THE BRUISED HEART AND THE TIRE IRON

I am aware that these things seem emotionally distant and unrelated to the personal pains of many. In our quiet daily miseries of marriage or parenting or loneliness or sickness or depression, we may feel that all this talk about the grandeur of God is like trying to heal a bruised heart with a tire iron. I know that God is tender, and that personal fellowship with him is sweet, and that touching the heart happens through the brokenness of the still, small voice. I know this, and I love it. Jesus Christ is a precious friend to me.

But I also know something else. If, while I am having a tender conversation with my wife, a man breaks in and kills her and all my children and leaves me wounded on the living room floor, I will need a way of seeing the world that involves more than the tenderness of God. If pestilence takes out tens of thousands of my fellow citizens and half my church, my mental and spiritual survival will depend on more than the precious gifts of God's intimacy.

CATASTROPHES ARE COMING

I am writing this book to build a vision of God into our lives that will not let us down in the worst of times. I mean really bad times. Horrific times. Who is prepared to meet the Agony that is coming?

Our worship services and our preaching too often pamper us. They coddle. I am not opposed to friends helping us with the daily frustrations that make us unhappy. There is plenty of proverbial wisdom in the Bible to warrant this. It is good. Love does this. I need this help. I want it. There is a time for everything under heaven, even pampering. But surely the preaching of God's word must aim for more than this.

Global cataclysms and personal catastrophes are coming. I say this not as one with my finger in the wind, but with my finger in the Bible. "Through many tribulations we must enter the kingdom of God" (Acts 14:22). "If they persecuted me, they will also persecute you" (John 15:20). "You yourselves know that we are destined for [these afflictions]" (1 Thess. 3:3). "All who desire to live a godly life in Christ Jesus will be persecuted" (2 Tim. 3:12). We are "fellow heirs with Christ, provided we suffer with him" (Rom. 8:17). "Not only the creation, but we ourselves, who have the firstfruits of the Spirit, groan inwardly as we wait eagerly for adoption as sons, the redemption of our bodies" (Rom. 8:23).

"YOUR BROTHER AND PARTNER IN THE TRIBULATION"

I have shepherded too many Christians through death in the best of times to think that any times are easy. But hard times are coming. Times are coming that have already been. Times when we will speak again the way John spoke on the island of Patmos. We will write to one another and, with no sense of melodrama, sign our letters, "Your brother and partner in the tribulation and the kingdom and the patient endurance that are in Jesus" (Rev. 1:9). Few write like this now in the West. But we will.

Times are coming when shepherds will say again to their flock, as they have done in days gone by, "Do not fear what you are about to suffer. Behold, the devil is about to throw some of you into prison, that you may be tested, and for ten days you will have tribulation. Be faithful unto death, and I will give you the crown of life" (Rev. 2:10). I am deeply thankful for Christian counseling to make my marriage better. But in addition, I need a shepherd who will tell me: "The devil may kill you, but that's okay. Jesus will give you the crown of life."

THE BEAST WILL WIN . . . FOR A SEASON

Along with the tender words of daily blessings, I need the tough warning that the Beast will win. For a season. "[The Beast] was allowed to make war on the saints and to conquer them . . . and . . . cause those who would not worship the image of the beast to be slain" (Rev. 13:7, 15). I need the warning that the great Babylonian whore will one day be "drunk with the blood of the saints, the blood of the martyrs of Jesus" (Rev. 17:6).

These horrors are in the Bible. God's word. Where is the shepherd who is preparing the saints for this kind of future? What answer could he give to our questions? What answer would fit with the upbeat entertainment mood? Where in the West do we hear the answer: "They have conquered him by the blood of the Lamb and by the word of their testimony, for they loved not their lives even unto death" (Rev. 12:11)?

OUR FELT NEEDS ARE ABOUT TO CHANGE

The fact that people do not feel a need for this kind of food in their spiritual diet should not silence the wise and loving shepherd. Our felt needs are about to change dramatically. Pastors will be glad if they are ahead of the curve. Otherwise, it may be too late. Coddled people will not be good listeners when their world collapses. They will be numb with confusion and rage at the God who wasn't supposed to allow this. "If this is the way God is, why didn't you tell us?"

The aim of this book is not to meet felt needs, but to awaken needs that will soon be felt, and then to save your faith and strengthen your courage when evil prevails. These are big, deep, weighty, strong truths. Truths for pestilence and war and personal calamity. These truths are made of steel. I know that a tire iron cannot caress a bruised heart, but if your car is rolling over on you and about to crush you, a cold, steel perpendicular tire iron might save your life. Then later, at home, as you tell the story, tears will flow, and Jesus will hold you as you sob for joy.

THE "SUCCESS" OF SIN IN THE PROVIDENCE OF GOD

My aim is to show that sin and evil, no matter how spectacular, never nullify the decisive, Christ-exalting purposes of God. No, my aim is more than that. These spectacular sins do not just *fail* to nullify God's purpose to glorify Christ, they *succeed*, by God's unfathomable providence, in making his gracious purpose come to pass. This truth is the steel God offers to put in the spine of his people as they face the worst calamities. There will be tenderness in due time. But if the back of our faith is broken because we think God is evil or absent, who will welcome him when he comes with caresses?

THE AIM IS LOVE

In the end, my aim, as I will make clear as we go along, is that you will be given the strength and courage of never-failing love toward all people, including your enemies (Matt. 5:43–44). "Love bears all things, believes all things, hopes all things, endures all things" (1 Cor. 13:7). There will be much to endure. Without a way of seeing the world that can deal with massive evil and unremitting pain under the supremacy of Christ, we will collapse in self-pity or rage. This is the opposite of love. If we are to endure and bear and believe and hope, we need to see the spectacular sins of history the way God sees them.

I hope this book helps. The assumption is that telling the stories of these sins as they are told in the Bible will be as helpful as writing a formal theology of providence. Once the stories are in place, you then have a lifetime to trace out all their implications in larger books than this.

HOW A LITTLE WINDOW WORKS

This book is small. But my prayers for it are large. Sometimes, if you put your eye close enough, the smallest pinhole can reveal a new world. It isn't the size of the window that determines how much you see. It's which way the window is facing, and how close you are, and whether the glass is clear. The little window of this book is facing toward the Son of God and the triumphs of his glory through some of the most spectacular sins of history. The glass I have used in building this window is the Bible. If I am not faithful to what the Christian Scriptures teach, you should take your leave. I hope that you will come close to the pane so that the fullest panorama is visible.

SPECTACULAR
SINS

1

GOD SOVEREIGN OVER HUMAN SIN

The Impulses Behind This Book

The king did not listen to the people, for it was a turn of affairs brought about by God.

CHRONICLES 10:15

"Now therefore behold, the LORD has put a lying spirit in the mouth of these your prophets. The LORD has declared disaster concerning you."

2 CHRONICLES 18:22

Amaziah would not listen, for it was of God, in order that he might give them into the hand of their enemies, because they had sought the gods of Edom.

2 CHRONICLES 25:20

The first impulse to write this book came when we were on vacation in 2007. I was sitting on a porch in Asheville, North Carolina. It was midsummer, and that means I was in 2 Chronicles. My through-the-Bible-in-a-year reading plan[1] had put me in the same place in the Bible that it does every summer. Reading the Bible with the same plan every year makes for some interesting associations in my mind between towns and texts. The association with Asheville that year was God's sovereignty over demonic evil and human sin.

---

[1]See www.hopeingod.org/BibleReadingPlan.aspx.

WHAT I SAW IN ASHEVILLE

Here's a glimpse of what I was seeing and what I mean by God's sovereignty over sin. I'm sitting there on the porch looking out over the Blue Ridge Mountains (and they really are blue at certain times of day), and I am reading things like this:

A Turn of Affairs Brought about by God

First, Solomon, king of Israel, had died. His son Rehoboam was about to be made king. Jeroboam, who had opposed Solomon and was driven into exile in Egypt, returned quickly and gathered the people behind him as a popular leader. He took the people and stood before Rehoboam and offered to serve him if he would lighten their load. "Your father made our yoke heavy. Now therefore lighten the hard service of your father and his heavy yoke on us, and we will serve you" (2 Chron. 10:4).

Rehoboam sought counsel from the old men. They counseled wisely, "If you will be good to this people and please them and speak good words to them, they will be your servants forever" (2 Chron. 10:7).

But Rehoboam abandoned the counsel of the old men and sought counsel from "the young men who had grown up with him." They gave foolish counsel: "Thus shall you speak to the people . . . 'My little finger is thicker than my father's thighs. And now, whereas my father laid on you a heavy yoke, I will add to your yoke. My father disciplined you with whips, but I will discipline you with scorpions'" (2 Chron. 10:10–11).

Rehoboam embraced the foolish counsel of the young men. The result was the tragic split of Israel into two warring kingdoms—ten tribes in the north and two tribes in the south. Why did Rehoboam react in this sinful and foolish way? There are layers of answers. But the writer of 2 Chronicles tells us the *ultimate* answer: "The king did not listen to the people, *for it was a turn of affairs brought about by God*" (2 Chron. 10:15).

This is what I mean by God's sovereignty over sin.

God Put a Lying Spirit in the Mouths of the Prophets

Second, a few chapters later Ahab, king of the northern tribes of Israel, made an alliance with Jehoshaphat, the king of the southern tribes. They would go to war together against Syria. Before going they sought counsel from the prophets. Four hundred prophets counseled them to go up against Syria. God would give it into their hands, they said (2 Chron. 18:11).

But these prophets were deceived. The one true prophet, Micaiah, described to the kings what had happened. He gave a window into heaven. He explained that among the hosts gathered before God there was a "lying spirit" who volunteered to deceive the prophets. "I will go out, and will be a lying spirit in the mouth of all his prophets" (2 Chron. 18:21). So God says, "You are to entice him, and you shall succeed; go out and do so." Then the true prophet Micaiah said to Ahab, "Now therefore behold, the Lord has put a lying spirit in the mouth of these your prophets. The Lord has declared disaster concerning you" (2 Chron. 18:22). Why did the prophets give false and destructive counsel to King Ahab? There are layers of answers. But the writer of 2 Chronicles gives the *ultimate* one: "The Lord has put a lying spirit in the mouth of these your prophets."

It Was of God

Third, one more illustration from what I was reading on the porch in Asheville. Seven chapters later in 2 Chronicles, Amaziah, the king of Judah, became bigheaded by a recent victory over the nation of Edom. In his pride, he decided to press his authority on the northern kingdom ruled by Joash.

Joash resisted and pointed out Amaziah's pride: "You say, 'See, I have struck down Edom,' and your heart has lifted you up in boastfulness." Then he gave him wise counsel: "Stay at home. Why should you provoke trouble so that you fall, you and Judah with you?" (2 Chron. 25:19).

But Amaziah would not forsake his pride and aggression.

Why? Again the answer has many layers. But the writer of 2 Chronicles gives us the *ultimate* answer: "Amaziah would not listen, *for it was of God*, in order that he might give them into the hand of their enemies, because they had sought the gods of Edom" (2 Chron. 25:20).

This is what I mean by the sovereignty of God over sin.[2]

THE IMPULSES GIVING RISE TO THIS BOOK

Why Does God Want Us to Know His Sovereignty over Sin?

Why does God think it is good for us to know this? Why does God tell us repeatedly in the Bible that, in some unfathomable way, he governs the sinful acts of men? We know that God him-

---

[2] I am aware that James 1:13–15 is a text some would use against this point. "Let no one say when he is tempted, 'I am being tempted by God,' for God cannot be tempted with evil, and he himself tempts no one. (14) But each person is tempted when he is lured [*exelkomenos*] and enticed [*deleazomenos*] by his own desire. (15) Then desire when it has conceived [*syllabousa*] gives birth [*tiktei*] to sin, and sin when is it is fully grown brings forth death." There is no point in hiding each other's problem texts. I am not allowed to pick and choose any more than I allow it to others. If I cannot make texts harmonize, I try to let them both stand until someone wiser than I can (even if I must wait for God's final enlightenment in heaven).

My effort at understanding James 1:13, in view of all the examples of God's willing that sinful actions come about, is to say that "tempt" is defined in verse 14 as being "dragged away" (*exelkomenos*) and "lured" (*deleazomenos*). In other words, James is not thinking of temptation in terms of an object of desire being put in front of someone (note that he does not attribute "temptation" to Satan, the arch-"tempter," but to our "desire"). For example, temptation is not the pornography on display, in James's way of thinking here; rather, it is the "dragging" and "luring" experienced in the heart that makes a person look at the pornography. He is thinking of temptation as *the engagement of the emotions in strong desires for evil*. This he calls the "conceiving" (*syllabousa*) stage of temptation before the actual "birth" (*tiktei*) of the *act* of sin (v. 15).

Thus it seems to me that James is saying that God never experiences this kind of "being dragged away" or "being lured." And he does not directly (see Chapter Four, note 1) produce that "dragging" and "luring" toward evil in humans. In some way (that we may not be able to fully comprehend), God is able without blameworthy "tempting" to see to it that a person does what God ordains for him to do even if it involves evil.

But when James says that God "cannot be tempted by evil," he is not saying that God cannot have objective enticements to evil put in front of him (for Jesus certainly was "tempted" in this sense in the wilderness), nor that he himself does not arrange events at times so that such enticements come before us, which may lead us, through the "dragging" of our desires, to sin (which God knew and, therefore, in one sense, willed). In fact, the Bible reveals that God tests (same word as "tempt" in Greek) his people often (cf. Heb. 11:17) by arranging their circumstances so that they are presented with dangerous acts of obedience that they might sinfully fear, or sinful pleasures that they might covet. In the end, what I say is that God is able to order events, if it seems wise and good to do so, such that sin comes about; yet he does so without "tempting" those who sin, as James says. See John Piper, "Are There Two Wills in God?" in Thomas R. Schreiner and Bruce Ware, eds. *Still Sovereign: Contemporary Perspectives on Election, Foreknowledge, and Grace* (Grand Rapids, MI: Baker Books, 2000), 107–131.

self never sins or does anything evil or unholy. If there is one thing the Bible is clear about, it is that God is holy and does not sin. "Holy, holy, holy, is the Lord God Almighty, who was and is and is to come!" (Rev. 4:8; see Isa. 6:3). "God is light, and in him is no darkness at all" (1 John 1:5). "God cannot be tempted with evil, and he himself tempts no one" (Jas. 1:13). "Shall not the Judge of all the earth do what is just?" (Gen. 18:25). Yes. That is not up for grabs. God is just and holy and eternally without sin.

So why does God tell us about his sovereignty over sin? It troubles people. Why does he want us to know this? There must be some good reason. I want to know what that is. That's the first impulse that gives rise to this book.

Why Does God Not Restrain Sin More Often?

The second impulse behind this book is the overwhelming evil in the world. Whatever month of the year you choose, heart-rending calamities fill the news from coast to coast and around the world. And if we had the connections to know about them, we would see that they fill our churches as well. Calamities strike the world of unbelievers and the children of God every day with mind-numbing pain. Some of these tragedies come directly from natural disasters, and some come directly from the sinful acts of man against man.

Just when you think violent crime in one state is decreasing, you read about a major city where the murder rate is up 50 percent in the last seven years. Just when you hear that drug use is on the decline among teenagers, you read about execution-style murders among our youth. Somewhere in the news miners are trapped deep underground, and family members are huddled in a church hoping against hope. An interstate bridge collapses, and a just-married husband doesn't arrive home for supper— ever. Planes collide, and bodies fall from the sky. Trains explode in flesh-burning balls of flame. The most stable countries suddenly burst into ethnic violence, and headlines venture the term *genocide*. A father throws his children off a bridge to spite his wife. Little girls are kidnapped and made to serve as sex slaves. Ethnic and religious minorities are systematically starved out of existence. Tsunamis sweep away whole villages and churches. Earthquakes bury thirty thousand people in a night. Suddenly twenty million people are displaced with South Asian flooding. And forty-six million pre-born babies are killed every year around the world.

Does this have anything to do with Jesus Christ—the risen king of the universe who stops the threatening wind and waves with a single word (Luke 8:24–25), who commands the dead and they live (John 11:43–44), who makes the lame walk and the blind see and the deaf hear (Matt. 11:5), who feeds five thousand with a few loaves of bread (Mark 6:41–42), who created the universe and everything in it (John 1:3), and who upholds the universe with the word of his power (Heb. 1:3) and says, "All authority in heaven and earth has been given to me" (Matt. 28:18)?

Surely, this Jesus can stop a tsunami, and make the wind blow a jet off its deadly course toward a crowded tower, and loosen the stranglehold of an umbilical cord from around an infant's neck, and blind the eyes of torturers, and stop a drought. Surely he can do this and a thousand other acts of restraint and rescue. He has done it before. He could do it now. What is his reason for not doing it more often than he does? That is the second impulse that gives rise to this book.

How Can We Have Faith and Joy during the Severity of the Last Days?

Third, the Bible itself tells us that in the last days things will be difficult and severe. There will be much suffering, and it will not exclude the followers of Jesus. In 2 Timothy 3:1 Paul says, "Understand this, that in the last days there will come *times of difficulty*." This statement is meant as a warning for Christians to expect trouble. Lots of trouble.

He goes on to explain that the source of this difficulty will be pervasive sin. "People will be lovers of self, lovers of money, proud, arrogant, abusive, disobedient to their parents, ungrateful, unholy, heartless, unappeasable, slanderous, without self-control, brutal, not loving good, treacherous, reckless, swollen with conceit, lovers of pleasure rather than lovers of God, having the appearance of godliness, but denying its power" (2 Tim. 3:2–5).

Together with human sinfulness, the last days will be permeated with natural calamities. It will be as though the earth is in the heavings of childbirth. "Nation will rise against nation, and kingdom against kingdom, and there will be famines and earthquakes in various places. All these are but the beginning of the birth pains" (Matt. 24:7–8).

There will be sweeping hostilities toward Christians: "They will deliver you up to tribulation and put you to death, and you will be hated by all nations for my name's sake" (Matt. 24:9). "Because lawlessness will be increased, the love of many will grow cold" (Matt. 24:12).

Tragedies and calamities and horrific suffering and sinful atrocities should not take Christians off guard. "Beloved, do not be surprised at the fiery trial when it comes upon you to test you, as though something strange were happening to you" (1 Pet. 4:12). They are foreseen by God, and he foretold them for us to know. God sees them coming and does not intend to stop them. Therefore, it appears that they somehow fit into his purposes.

Indeed, he says as much about the murder of his saints in Revelation 6:10–11. Those who had already been killed cry out in heaven, "O Sovereign Lord, holy and true, how long before you will judge and avenge our blood on those who dwell on the earth?" John describes the answer they receive: "They were each given a white robe and told to rest a little longer, *until the number of their fellow servants and their brothers should be complete, who were to be killed* as they themselves had been."

There is a number of martyrs to be filled. God knows how many murders of his children there must be. And God reigns over every one of them. He does not spare his children physical death, but he does save them eternally: "Some of you they will put to death. . . . But not a hair of your head will perish" (Luke 21:16, 18).

As a pastor, I do not think it is my job to entertain you during the last days. It is not my calling to help you have chipper feelings while the whole creation groans. My job is to put the kind of ballast in the belly of your boat so that when these waves crash against your life, you will not capsize but make it to the harbor of heaven—battered and wounded, but full of faith and joy. That's the third impulse that gives rise to this book.

How Is Christ Glorified in a World of Sin?

The fourth impulse behind this book is the ultimate aim of my life and ministry. Recently I went back almost three decades and listened to my candidating sermon at the church I still serve. It was January 27, 1980. I told that old and graying downtown church that I had one supreme passion and one simple goal. I learned it from my father, and I learned it from the apostle Paul.

I exist to magnify Jesus Christ. That is, I am on this planet for one ultimate reason: to do whatever I can to make Jesus Christ known and treasured—a knowing and a treasuring that accords with his infinite beauty and immeasurable worth. My text that Sunday was the clearest statement of this passion and goal in the Bible. The text was Philippians 1:20: "It is my eager expectation and hope that I will not be at all ashamed, but that with full courage now as always *Christ will be magnified in my body, whether by life or by death.*" Paul's "eager expectation" is that Christ be made to look as great as he really is by the way Paul lives and dies. That's my passion too.

This is the fourth impulse behind this book. How is Christ magnified in a world like ours? Or a world like 2 Chronicles? How is Christ magnified in the fall of Satan from his position of perfection? In the sin of Adam and the fall of the entire human race into sin and misery? In the tower of Babel and the fracturing of the human race into thousands of languages? In the sale of Joseph into slavery in Egypt? In Israel's treason against God in demanding a human king to be like the nations? In the betrayal of the Son of God by the kiss of his friend?

SORROWFUL, YET ALWAYS REJOICING

Between Asheville and this book, I preached a series of messages under the title "Spectacular Sins and Their Global Purpose in the Glory of Christ." It marked the beginning of my twenty-eighth year of preaching at Bethlehem Baptist Church. There was death that autumn, just like there had been death in the spring. My father and my granddaughter. The I-35 bridge over the Mississippi River collapsed. Darkness overcame the young. And steady-state suffering kept its inexorable pace. I write out of the way I experience the word of God. And what I experience almost every day is someone's pain. Sometimes my own. Always someone else's that, in part, becomes mine.

We are Christian Hedonists at Bethlehem. That means we believe and pursue the truth that God is most glorified in us when we are most satisfied in him. But we also know that in this life, joy in God is never unmixed with sorrow. Never. Love won't allow that. Our banner bears the seal of 2 Corinthians 6:10, "sorrowful yet always rejoicing." We are pushing our way through a blood-spattered life that makes us feel connected to the world and disconnected at the same time. We are here but not here. Love binds us to the tragic earth, and love binds us to the Treasure of heaven. Christians are strange. Our emotions are inexplicable in ordinary terms. "[Let] those who [mourn] mourn as though they were not mourning, and those who [rejoice] rejoice as though they were not rejoicing" (1 Cor. 7:30). That is our experience. That is the daily context of this book.

2

CHRIST SOVEREIGN OVER ALL HOSTILE POWERS

All Things Were Created for Him

He is the image of the invisible God, the firstborn of all creation. For by him all things were created, in heaven and on earth, visible and invisible, whether thrones or dominions or rulers or authorities—all things were created through him and for him.

COLOSSIANS 1:15–16

God has not answered all of our questions about the sin and misery that are in the world. "The secret things belong to the LORD our God" (Deut. 29:29). There are mysteries we will not fathom while "we see in a mirror dimly" (1 Cor. 13:12). In this present age, we "know in part"; in the age to come we will know even as we are known (1 Cor. 13:12).

But God has not been silent about these things. There are things he wants us to know. The honor of his Son is at stake in the spectacular sins of history and their global purpose in the glory of Christ. The apostle Paul makes this clear in Colossians 1:9–20.

THE MOST CONCENTRATED DESCRIPTION OF CHRIST'S GLORIES

Paul has just prayed for the Colossians that they would "be filled with the knowledge of [God's] will in all spiritual wisdom and understanding, so as to walk in a manner worthy of the Lord, fully pleasing to him, bearing fruit in every good work and increasing in the knowledge of God" (Col. 1:9–10). In verse 14, he begins a litany of amazing truths about Jesus Christ that are probably the most concentrated description of the glories of Jesus in the entire Bible. I will mention them—all fifteen of them—and then come back to the one I want to focus on.

- In him we have redemption, the forgiveness of sins (v. 14).
- He is the image of the invisible God (v. 15a).
- He is the firstborn of all creation—that is, the specially honored, first and only Son over all creation (v. 15b).
- By him all things were created, in heaven and on earth, visible and invisible, whether thrones or dominions or rulers or authorities (v. 16a).
- All things were created through him (v. 16b).
- All things were created for him (v. 16c).
- He is before all things (v. 17a).
- In him all things hold together (v. 17b).
- He is the head of the body, the church (v. 18a).
- He is the beginning (v. 18b).
- He is the firstborn from the dead (v. 18c).
- In everything he is preeminent (v. 18d).
- In him all the fullness of God was pleased to dwell (v. 19).
- He reconciles all things to himself, whether on earth or in heaven (v. 20a).
- He makes peace by the blood of his cross (v. 20b).

This is worth memorizing. If your heart ever wavers and grows cold, come here. Memorize this litany of glories, and ask God to give you affections that correspond to the measure of this greatness—infinite in beauty, immeasurable. If any person or any power or any wisdom or any love awakens any admiration or any amazement or any joy, let it be the greatest person and the greatest power and the greatest wisdom and the greatest love that exists—Jesus Christ.

ALL THINGS CREATED BY, THROUGH, AND FOR JESUS CHRIST

But for our purposes in this book, we go back to verse 16. Notice the three prepositions: "For *by* him all things were created . . . all things were created *through* him and *for* him." So Paul teaches us that Jesus Christ created all that is. They were created *through* him. And all things were created *for* him.

All that came into being exists for Christ—that is, everything exists to display the greatness of Christ. Nothing—nothing!—in the universe exists for its own sake. Everything—from the bottom of the oceans to the top of the mountains, from the smallest particle to the biggest star, from the most boring school subject to the most fascinating science, from the ugliest cockroach to the most beautiful human, from the greatest saint to the most wicked genocidal dictator—everything that exists, exists to make the greatness of Christ more fully known—including *you*, and the person you have the hardest time liking.

EVEN EVIL SUPERNATURAL POWERS

But of all the things—the millions of things Paul could have mentioned that Christ made and that exist for his glory—he chose to mention these: thrones, dominions, rulers, and authorities. Verse 16: "For by him all things were created, in heaven and on earth, visible and invisible, whether *thrones or dominions or rulers or authorities*—[even these] were created through him and for him."

Now Paul knows that these "rulers" and "authorities" include evil supernatural powers. We can see this in the next chapter. In Colossians 2:15, Paul celebrates Jesus' triumph on the cross by saying, "He disarmed the *rulers and authorities* and put them to open shame, by triumphing over them in him." So here are the "rulers and authorities" that he referred to in Colossians 1:16. They are evil. Jesus died to disarm them.

They turn up again in Ephesians 6:12: "We do not wrestle against flesh and blood, but *against the rulers, against the authorities.*" They are, Paul says, "the cosmic powers over this present darkness . . . the spiritual forces of evil in the heavenly places." They are evil supernatural powers that aim to deceive and destroy the human race.

According to Colossians 2:15, they have been decisively defeated at the cross where Jesus disarmed them and made his believing people completely secure. But they still do much harm in the world because not everyone believes, and even believers can be hurt by them, but not destroyed.

For example, Jesus said to the church in Smyrna, "Do not fear what you are about to suffer. Behold, the devil is about to throw some of you into prison, that you may be tested, and for ten days you will have tribulation. Be faithful unto death, and I will give you the crown of life" (Rev. 2:10). The devil can imprison and kill God's loved ones. But he cannot destroy them. That is the kind of power the rulers and authorities have.

FOR THE GLORY OF JESUS CHRIST

So where do these evil supernatural powers come from and why do they exist? Colossians 1:16 gives a decisive part of the answer. Not the whole answer, but the part we need to know. They come from Christ. "By him [by Christ, the Son of God!] all things were created, in heaven and on earth, visible and invisible, whether thrones or dominions or *rulers or authorities.* . . ." That's where they came from. They were created by Christ. And why do they exist? Verse 16b: "All things were created through him and *for* him." They exist *for* Christ. They exist to make his glories known—to display his infinite beauty and immeasurable worth.

It doesn't say he created them *evil*. In fact, the little New Testament book of Jude speaks of "angels who did not stay within their own position of authority, but left their proper dwelling" (Jude 6). They were created good, and they rebelled against God.

Paul knows this. He knows what they once *were* and what they *have become*. And we will see in the chapters to come that Paul knows something else. He knows that Christ knew they would fall before they fell. Christ knew that there would be sin and rebellion and evil. And with infinite wisdom he and his Father took it all into account as they planned the history of salvation and the triumphs of grace at Calvary.

Therefore, when Paul says, "rulers [and] authorities" were created by Christ and for Christ, he means that they were created knowing what they would become and how it is that precisely in that evil role they would glorify Christ—knowing everything they would become, they were created for the glory of Christ.

FUEL FOR A GOD-CENTERED FIRE

Now why would Paul tell us this? Is it helpful to know this? Paul certainly thinks so, because these evil powers are the one thing Paul chooses to mention as an example of what was created by Christ and for Christ. Of all the thousands of things he could have mentioned, he mentions these evil powers. He wants us to know this. Why? Why does he think this is good for us to know? That's what this book is about.

The main point of this book is not information for your heads, but application to your lives. I am thinking as I write of the way Paul was thinking about Timothy as he wrote his second letter to Timothy. In dealing with an intensely practical, and probably painful, matter in Timothy's life, Paul leads him back to the most profound, and even mind-boggling, doctrinal truth. Timothy is prone to anxiety. He is retiring and sometimes fearful. His timidity threatens the effectiveness of his ministry.

Paul wants to help him overcome his fear and be courageous. So Paul says, "Do not be ashamed of the testimony about our Lord, nor of me his prisoner, but share in suffering for the gospel by the power of God" (2 Tim. 1:8). That much we may expect. But then to help Timothy even more, he takes him into heavy theology.

He describes God in the next verse like this: ". . . [God] saved us and called us to a holy calling, not because of our works but because of his own purpose and *grace, which he gave us in Christ Jesus before the ages began.*" Paul tells timid Timothy that before there was any human sin in the world that needed grace, before Adam had sinned, before the world existed, God gave grace to Timothy in Christ Jesus for salvation. God had Timothy in view, and he had Jesus Christ in view, and he had grace in view, and he had salvation in view before there was any world or any human sin or any human guilt. That is heavy.

And why does he say it? Because Timothy is timid. Paul's antidote for wimpy Christians is weighty doctrine. In Paul's mind, the most massive truths are meant for producing radical lives of obedience. That's why I say the *main* point of this book is not information for your head, but application to your life. There is truth. Weighty truth like the kind Paul unveiled for Timothy in 2 Timothy 1:9. But the aim is love and justice and purity and compassion and courage. All to the end that Christ might be known and treasured as infinitely beautiful and immeasurably valuable. Great biblical truths are fuel in the fire of the God-centered soul.

WHY THE TRUTH OF CHRIST'S SOVEREIGNTY?

In anticipation of what is coming, we will end this chapter with five summary statements about why God wants us to know the truth of Christ's sovereignty over "rulers [and] authorities" and the way they are involved in the most spectacular sins of the universe—as well as all the others. God's sovereignty over sin in Jesus Christ is important to know for at least these five reasons.

First, God wants us to know this because *it is objectively true, not merely opinion or a merely human idea.* It is a fact. It is real, like the seat you are sitting on. Or the floor on which you stand. Or the mattress where you lie. Truth matters. People perish, Paul says, for not knowing and loving the truth. His heart aches for those "who are perishing, because they refused to love the truth and so be saved" (2 Thess. 2:10).

Second, God wants us to know this truth because *it makes clear that Christ alone, not "rulers [and] authorities," is to be worshipped.* Some people in Colossae were saying that the "worship of angels" (Col. 2:18) was part of the way up to God. No, Paul says, these angels that some think are so great—the good ones and the evil ones—were created by Christ and for Christ. Don't worship them. Worship the one who made them.

Third, God wants us to know these things because *our day is not so unlike Paul's. Paul was concerned that, in the pluralistic, intellectual atmosphere of Colossae, Christians could be captivated by high-sounding heresies.* "See to it that no one takes you captive by philosophy and empty deceit, according to human tradition, according to the elemental spirits of the world, and not according to Christ" (Col. 2:8). Paul believed that the great truth of Christ's sovereignty over sin and evil was a kind of ballast in our boats that would keep us from capsizing under the waves of error that roll endlessly over the sea of human culture. He believed that great truth would protect us from philosophies and traditions that do not cherish the supremacy of Christ. When you embrace truths like this, you are not easily swept away by man-centered trends or traditions.

Fourth, God wants us to know this truth *to make us valiant in the face of odds that seem overwhelming to the natural eye.* Paul wants to make crystal-clear that when Christians, who feel small and vulnerable, hear about hostile "thrones or dominions or rulers or authorities," they know beyond any doubt that Jesus Christ has all authority over them. He means to give us courage that these hostile powers cannot do anything apart from God's sovereign permission (Job 1:12; Luke 22:31–32).

And therefore, finally, Paul tells us these things because *he wants us to see and feel that our salvation in Christ is invincible.* When Christ died for sin and rose again, "he disarmed the rulers and authorities" (Col. 2:15). If you have put your trust in him, here is what he says about you in Colossians 3:3–4: "You have died, and your life is hidden with Christ in God. When Christ who is your life appears, then you also will appear with him in glory." You are secure forever in Christ. Nothing can separate you from him, not even the most vicious cosmic powers (Rom. 8:38–39).

ALL THINGS SERVE HIS GLORY AND OUR GLADNESS

All things were created *by* him and *through* him and *for* him— even our worst supernatural enemies. In the end, it was they—not Christ—who were shamed at the cross (Col. 2:15). In the end, everything and everyone serves to magnify the glory of our Savior and increase the gladness of his people in him.

3

THE FALL OF SATAN
AND THE VICTORY
OF CHRIST

Why Does God Permit Satan to Live?

God did not spare angels when they sinned, but cast them into hell and committed them to chains of gloomy darkness to be kept until the judgment.
2 PETER 2:4

"I will put enmity between you and the woman, and between your offspring and her offspring; he shall bruise your head, and you shall bruise his heel."
GENESIS 3:15

The devil who had deceived them was thrown into the lake of fire and sulfur where the beast and the false prophet were, and they will be tormented day and night forever and ever.
REVELATION 20:10

Vying for the most spectacular sin ever committed is the desire of once-holy angels to love their own glory more than God's. It is unfathomable. The Bible does not take us deep into the heart of such mysterious sin to explain the soul-dynamics that make rebellion rise out of righteousness. We are not given the final answer of how the origin of sin in the soul of a holy being takes place. But neither are we left to wonder if God was surprised or if he had to revamp all his plans. We are taken by Scripture deep into the halls of eternity and given glimpses that are breathtaking. And God's aim in this is not to promote speculation, but to awaken worship and make us mighty for Christ in the midst of sin and misery.

As we come through Genesis 1–2 to Genesis 3, all is well, it seems. Genesis 1:31 says, "God saw everything that he had made, and behold, it was very good." God did not create anything evil. It was all very good.

Then suddenly when chapter 3 opens, there is this serpent. And he is clearly evil. He is calling God's word into question. Verse 1: "Did God actually say, 'You shall not eat of any tree in the garden'?" He is devious and deceitful and destructive. God had said in Genesis 2:17, "The day that you eat of [this tree] you shall surely die." But the serpent says in verse 4: "You will not surely die. For God knows that when you eat of it your eyes will be opened, and you will be like God, knowing good and evil."

Therefore, Jesus says of him in John 8:44 that he is both a "liar" and a "murderer." "He was a murderer from the beginning, and has nothing to do with the truth, because there is no truth in him. When he lies, he speaks out of his own character, for he is a liar and the father of lies."

SATAN, THAT ANCIENT SERPENT

Who is this serpent? The fullest answer is given in Revelation 12:9: "The great dragon was thrown down, that ancient serpent, who is called the devil and Satan, the deceiver of the whole world—he was thrown down to the earth, and his angels were thrown down with him." So the serpent in the garden is *the devil* (which means *slanderer*), and *Satan* (which means *accuser*), and the deceiver of the whole world.

Jesus calls him "the evil one" (Matt. 13:19) and "the ruler of this world" (John 12:31; 14:30; 16:11). The Pharisees call him

"Beelzebul, the prince of demons" (Matt. 12:24). Paul calls him "the god of this world" (2 Cor. 4:4) and "the prince of the power of the air" (Eph. 2:2).

That's the one we meet in Genesis 3. He is already evil, already a deceiver, already a murderer when he appears in the garden of God. In Genesis 3:15, after the serpent lures Adam and Eve into sin, God pronounces judgment on the serpent: "I will put enmity between you and the woman, and between your offspring and her offspring; he shall bruise your head, and you shall bruise his heel."

Notice that at first it looks like the warfare will be between two offsprings: "between your offspring and her offspring." But in the next statement, something surprising is said: "He shall bruise your head." Who is *he*? Answer: the woman's offspring. Who is *your* ("he shall bruise *your* head")? Answer: the serpent himself, *not* his offspring. That is significant.

THE CRUSHING OF SATAN AT THE CROSS

The day is coming, God says, when *you*, the serpent (not just your offspring), will be defeated and removed from the earth. The offspring of this woman will crush you. That's why the Son of God became human. It was a human who would crush Satan—the seed of the woman.

Hebrews 2:14 describes the connection between the humanity of Jesus and the destruction of Satan. "Since therefore the children share in flesh and blood, he himself likewise partook of the same things, that through death he might destroy the one who has the power of death, that is, the devil." The decisive blow was struck by the perfect offspring of the woman, Jesus Christ, when he died on the cross. This is one of the reasons why the eternal Son of God had to become human—because it was the offspring of the woman who would crush Satan. "The reason the Son of God appeared was to destroy the works of the devil" (1 John 3:8). God intended for his Son to get the glory as the Victor over the serpent.

Colossians 2:14–15 describes what God did to the demons when his Son died on the cross: "The record of debt that stood against us . . . he set aside, nailing it to the cross. He disarmed the rulers and authorities and put them to open shame, by triumphing over them in him." When Christ died for our sins, Satan was disarmed and defeated. The one eternally destructive weapon that he had was stripped from his hand—namely, his accusation before God that we are guilty and should perish with him. When Christ died for us, that accusation was nullified.

All of us who entrust ourselves to Christ will never perish. No accusation will stand against us. Satan cannot separate you from the love of God in Christ (Rom. 8:37–39).

THE INSURRECTION OF SATAN

Now the question that cries out for an answer is: Where did Satan come from? And why does God tolerate his murderous activity? In Genesis 3, he just seems to appear. God created everything good, but something happened. The good creation was corrupted.

The books of Jude and 2 Peter in the New Testament give us clues as to what happened. Jude 6 says, "The angels who did not stay within their own position of authority, but left their proper dwelling, he has kept in eternal chains under gloomy darkness until the judgment of the great day." And 2 Peter 2:4 says, "God did not spare angels when they sinned, but cast them into hell and committed them to chains of gloomy darkness to be kept until the judgment."

This may not be a direct reference to the original fall of Satan and his rebellion. Some argue that it refers to the sins of angels ("sons of God") in Genesis 6:1–4. But in any case it is the best pointer we have in the Bible to how Satan and his subordinates came to be what they are.[1]

---

[1]Thomas Schreiner, for example, thinks the main reference of 2 Peter 2:4 and Jude 6 is to the sins of angels in Genesis 6:1–4 but says that the "prehistoric fall of angels" is "a legitimate deduction theologically." *1, 2 Peter, Jude*, The New American Commentary, Vol. 37 (Nashville: Broadman & Holman, 2003), 336.

It appears then that at first there was a host of holy angels. And some of them, including Satan, "sinned," or as Jude 6 says, "did not stay within their own position of authority." In other words, the sin was a kind of insurrection. A desire for more power and more authority than they were appointed to have *by* God and *under* God.

So Satan originates as a created angel who, with other angels, rebels against God. They reject him as their all-satisfying king and joy and set out on a course of self-exaltation and presumed self-determination. They do not want to be subordinate. They do not want to be sent by God to serve others (Heb. 1:14). They lose their reverence and admiration and satisfaction in God. Now they dream of having authority over themselves and exalting themselves above God.

THE ORIGIN OF SATAN'S SIN

But now we ask: Why? How could this happen? There is no easy answer. In fact, the ultimate biblical answer creates even more questions. So it seems that in this age, while we "know in part" (1 Cor. 13:12), not all our questions will be answered.

Some people find help in saying that the angels had "free will," and therefore God, out of respect for this free will, could not exert decisive influence to hold their allegiance or keep them adoring him. But I don't find that idea helpful. It simply doesn't answer the question: Why would a perfectly holy angel in God's infinitely beautiful presence use his free will to suddenly hate God?

This idea that God was unable to prevent the rebellion because of his respect for the innate self-determining wills of sinless angels is not a solution to the problem. It doesn't account for why perfectly holy beings would use their wills to despise what they were adoring when created. And it doesn't fit with what the rest of the Bible says about God's rule over the devil. In this setting, the term *free will* is simply another way of naming the mystery. But it's not the way the Bible deals with the situation.

My approach to answering the question of how to think about the origin of Satan's sin is to read the whole Bible with the question: How does God relate to Satan's will? Is God helpless before the will of evil powers? Is he respectful of the freedom of Satan's will so that he does not intrude on it and exert his sovereignty over it? Are there powers outside himself that limit his rule over them? Or is God presented throughout the Bible as having the right and the power to restrain Satan anytime he pleases? And if so, why doesn't he do it more often? In fact, why doesn't he just nullify him or destroy him entirely?

So when I read the Bible, here is what I find. Here are just a few glimpses of God's power over Satan. They point the way for how we should think about what measure of freedom Satan has.

GOD'S SOVEREIGN SWAY OVER SATAN

1. Though Satan is called "the ruler of this world" (John 12:31), Daniel 4:17 says, "The Most High [God] rules the kingdom of men and gives it to whom he will." And Psalm 33:10–11 says, "The LORD brings the counsel of the nations to nothing; he frustrates the plans of the peoples. The counsel of the LORD stands forever, the plans of his heart to all generations." Yes, Satan is "the ruler of this world" in a subordinate sense. God has given him astonishing latitude to work his sin and misery in the world. He is a great ruler over the world, but not the *ultimate* one. God holds the decisive sway.

2. Though unclean spirits are everywhere doing deceptive and murderous things, Jesus Christ has all authority over them. Mark 1:27 says, "He commands even the unclean spirits, and they obey him." When Christ commands the devil, the devil obeys. This raises the question about the difference between the command of God, say in the Ten Commandments, and the command of Christ in telling demons to depart or telling the universe to come into being. Clearly, God does exert his authority in giving

the Ten Commandments. All his creatures are obliged to obey, including the devil.

Nevertheless, the devil disobeys these commands every day. The authority that they have is not the same kind of authority that Jesus wields in Mark 1:27: "He commands even the unclean spirits, and they obey him." This is an absolute, *effective* authority. When God exerts this authority, it produces what it demands. When he wills, he can make the demons do what he commands.

This is a different authority than he exercises in his written law, such as the Ten Commandments. It is decisive. Christ holds sway over Satan's will whenever he pleases. This means that anytime demons are doing horrible things, Jesus is not commanding them to do otherwise. And in not commanding them to do otherwise, he has a reason for letting them do what they are doing.

3. Satan is a roaring lion, prowling and seeking to devour. Peter says, "Resist him, firm in your faith, knowing that the same experiences of *suffering* are being experienced by your brethren throughout the world" (1 Pet. 5:8–9). In other words, "suffering" is the way Satan is trying to devour the saints. But Peter says in 1 Peter 3:17, "It is better to *suffer* for doing good, *if that should be God's will*, than for doing evil." *If that should be God's will.* In other words, whether we suffer—whether the jaws of the lion are allowed to clamp down on our leg or throat—is ultimately decided by God. If the Lord wills, we will suffer or not. If the Lord wills, Satan will be given this permission or not. This suffering, these jaws of the prowling lion, are opened and closed only according to God's will. God holds final sway, not Satan.

4. Yes, Satan is a murderer from the beginning, Jesus said (John 8:44). But has Satan taken the gift of life out of the hand of the Giver? No. Deuteronomy 32:39 says, "See now that I, even I am he, and there is no god beside me; I kill and I *make alive*; I wound and I heal; and there is none that can deliver out of my hand." God holds final sway in every death and every life.

James says the same thing in James 4:15: "If the Lord wills, *we will live* and also do this or that." James does not say we will live "if *Satan* wills." He says, "If the Lord wills, we will live." The Lord gives, and the Lord takes away. And his name is blessed (Job 1:21). Satan is a murderer. But his choices whom to murder do not make the life-giving God his lackey. God makes all the final choices concerning who will live and who will die. Satan is not absolute. God is.

5. When Satan aims to destroy Job and prove that God is not his treasure, he must get permission from God before he attacks Job's possessions and his family with destruction, and before he attacks his body with sickness. In Job 1:12, God says to Satan, "Behold, all that [Job] has is in your hand. Only against him do not stretch out your hand." That is, "You have my permission to attack, but you will not go beyond the bounds that I set."

In Job 2:6 God gives Satan permission to go so far and no farther: "The LORD said to Satan, 'Behold, he is in your hand; only spare his life.'" And when the story is complete and the inspired writer is summarizing all that happened, he does not even give Satan so much as a mention. He sees only God's overarching supreme hand in all that Satan did: "[Job's brothers and sisters] showed him sympathy and comforted him for *all the evil that the LORD had brought upon him*" (Job 42:11). Satan's causality in all Job's suffering was not ultimate. That is why the writer can simply leave him out of account and say that the Lord was the final and decisive wisdom that ordered these things. Satan was not ultimate. God was.

6. Satan is the great tempter. He wants us to sin. Luke tells us that Satan was behind Peter's denials. He tempted him to deny Jesus. But could he do that without God's permission? Listen to what Jesus says to Simon Peter in Luke 22:31–32. It is very similar to the way Satan and God interact in Job: "Simon, Simon, behold, Satan has demanded to . . . sift you like wheat, but I have prayed for you, that your faith may not fail. And when you have turned again, strengthen your brothers."

Satan could not do what he wished with Peter without God's permission. And when he had it, just as with Job, God had set him a boundary: "You will *not* destroy Peter. You will only make him stumble tonight." Which is why Jesus says, "*When* [not *if*!] you have turned again, strengthen your brothers." Jesus, not Satan, has the upper hand here. And Satan is allowed to go so far and no farther.

7. Paul says in 2 Corinthians 4:4 that "the god of this world has blinded the minds of the unbelievers." But is this power to blind people an ultimate power? Can God overcome it and resist and nullify it? Yes, he can. Two verses later Paul says, "God, who said, 'Let light shine out of darkness,' has shone in our hearts to give the light of the knowledge of the glory of God in the face of Jesus Christ." In other words, the blinding effect of Satan gives way to God's light when he says, "Let there be light."

GOD GOVERNS SATAN'S EVERY MOVE

So now back to the question about the origin of Satan's sinfulness. Is God unable to do with his own angels what he does with the demons on earth: "He commands . . . and they obey" (Mark 1:27)? Is there a power outside himself that limits his rule over them? My conclusion is that from cover to cover the Bible presents God as governing Satan and his demons. He has the right and power to restrain them anytime he pleases. He holds sway over their wills. He commands the evil spirits, and they obey. I have no reason from the Bible to think otherwise.

I conclude, therefore, that God permitted Satan's fall, not because he was unable to stop it, but because he had a purpose for it. Since God is never taken off guard, his permissions are always purposeful. If he chooses to permit something, he does so for a reason—an infinitely wise reason because he is infinitely wise.

How the sin arises in Satan's heart, we do not know. God has not told us. What we do know is that God is sovereign over Satan, and therefore Satan's will does not move without God's permission. And therefore every move of Satan is part of God's overall purpose and plan. And this is true in such a way that God never sins. God is infinitely holy, and God is infinitely mighty. Satan is evil, and Satan is under the all-governing wisdom of God.

WHY NOT WIPE OUT SATAN?

Why, then, does God not simply wipe Satan out? He has the right and power to do this. And Revelation 20:10 says he is going to do it someday. "The devil who had deceived them was thrown into the lake of fire and sulfur where the beast and the false prophet were, and they will be tormented day and night forever and ever." Why didn't God cast him into the lake of fire the day after he rebelled? Why let him rampage through humanity for centuries?

Satan deserved the lake of fire the moment he rebelled against God. It is an infinitely grievous sin to rebel against an infinitely worthy Being. He was completely worthy of the lake of fire the moment he sinned. A finite number of sins following this rebellion would not bring Satan's guilt finally to the point of deserving the lake of fire. Satan did not need millennia of sinful carnage to deserve the lake of fire. God had the right and the power to put Satan out of commission the moment he sinned. Therefore, the fact that God did not do it shows that he had a reason. Can we know what it was?

FOR THE FULLNESS OF CHRIST'S GLORY

The ultimate answer, as we saw in the last chapter, is that "all things were created through [Christ] and for [Christ]" (Col. 1:16). God foresaw all that Satan would do if he created Satan and permitted him to rebel. In choosing to create him, he was choosing to fold all of that evil into his purpose for creation. That purpose for creation was the glory of his Son. All things, including Satan and all his followers, were created with this in view. They were created knowing what they would do, and that knowledge was taken into account in God's decision to create them. Therefore, the evil that they do in the world is part of how the greatest purpose of God will be accomplished.

Satan's fall and ongoing existence are for the glory of Christ. The Son of God, Jesus Christ, will be more highly honored and more deeply appreciated and loved in the end because he defeats Satan not the moment after Satan fell, but through millennia of long-suffering, patience, humility, servanthood, suffering, and decisively through his own death. A single, sudden, and infinitely holy display of power to destroy Satan immediately after his fall would have been a glorious display of power and righteousness. But it would not have been the fullest possible display of all the glories in the Son and the Father. God chose an infinitely wise way of displaying the full array of divine glories in letting Satan fall and do his work for millennia.

The glory of Christ reaches its highest point in the obedient sacrifice of the cross where Jesus triumphed over the devil (Col. 2:15). Jesus said in that final hour of his own sacrifice, "Now is the Son of Man glorified, and God is glorified in him" (John 13:31). Paul said that the crucifixion of Christ is the point where we see his wisdom and power most gloriously displayed: "We preach Christ crucified . . . the power of God and the wisdom of God" (1 Cor. 1:23–24).

Jesus said to Paul about Satan's thorn in Paul's side, "My power is made perfect in weakness" (2 Cor. 12:9). Satan, and all his pain, serves in the end to magnify the power and wisdom and love and grace and mercy and patience and wrath of Jesus Christ. We would not know Christ in the fullness of his glory if he had not defeated Satan in the way he did.

HOW TO RELATE TO EVIL

So I close this chapter with an urgent and practical question: How then should we relate to evil? How should we think and feel and act about satanic evil? The death of a little boy at the attack of a pit bull? The deaths of three valiant miners trying to save their buddies? Five hundred dead in an earthquake in Peru? These are just some of the agonies in the news the week I preached this message. And what about the evil and pain you confront in your own lives? Here is my summary answer.

Eight Things to Do with Evil

On the one hand:

1. *Expect* evil. "Do not be surprised at the fiery trial when it comes upon you to test you, as though something strange were happening to you" (1 Pet. 4:12).

2. *Endure* evil. "Love bears all thing, believes all things, hopes all things, endures all things" (1 Cor. 13:7; cf. Mark 13:13).

3. *Give thanks* for the refining effect of evil that comes against you. "Give thanks always and for everything to God the Father in the name of our Lord Jesus Christ" (Eph. 5:20; cf. 1 Thess. 5:18). "We rejoice in our sufferings, knowing that suffering produces endurance . . ." (Rom. 5:3–5).

4. *Hate* evil. "Let love be genuine. *Abhor* what is evil; hold fast to what is good" (Rom. 12:9).

5. *Pray for escape* from evil. "Lead us not into temptation, but deliver us from evil" (Matt. 6:13).

6. *Expose* evil. "Take no part in the unfruitful works of darkness, but instead expose them" (Eph. 5:11).

7. *Overcome* evil with good. "Do not be overcome by evil, but overcome evil with good" (Rom. 12:21).

8. *Resist* evil. "Resist the devil and he will flee from you" (Jas. 4:7).

Four Things Never to Do with Evil

But on the other hand:

1. *Never despair* that this evil world is out of God's control.

"[He] works all things according to the counsel of his will" (Eph. 1:11).

2. *Never give in* to the sense that because of seemingly random evil, life is absurd and meaningless. "How unsearchable are his judgments and how inscrutable his ways! . . . For from him and through him and to him are all things. To him be glory forever" (Rom. 11:33, 36).

3. *Never yield* to the thought that God sins or is ever unjust or unrighteous in the way he governs the universe. "The LORD is righteous in all his ways" (Ps. 145:17).

4. *Never doubt* that God is totally *for you* in Christ. If you trust him with your life, you are in Christ. Never doubt that all the evil that befalls you—even if it takes your life—is God's loving, purifying, saving, fatherly discipline. It is not an expression of his punishment in wrath. That wrath fell on Jesus Christ our substitute (Gal. 3:13; Rom. 8:3). Only mercy comes to us from God, not wrath, if we are his children through faith in Jesus. "The Lord disciplines the one he loves, and chastises every son whom he receives" (Heb. 12:6).

When we renounce the designs of the devil and trust the power and wisdom and goodness of God displayed in the humble triumphs of Jesus Christ, we fulfill God's purpose in letting Satan live a little longer. We glorify the infinitely superior worth of Jesus. So I invite you to trust him and to stand in awe of how he saves you and defeats Satan in one great sacrifice of love.

4

THE FATAL DISOBEDIENCE OF ADAM AND THE TRIUMPHANT OBEDIENCE OF CHRIST

How Adam's Sin Serves the Supremacy of Christ

Death reigned from Adam to Moses, even over those whose sinning was not like the transgression of Adam, who was a type of the one who was to come.
ROMANS 5:14

If, because of one man's trespass, death reigned through that one man, much more will those who receive the abundance of grace and the free gift of righteousness reign in life through the one man Jesus Christ.
ROMANS 5:17

One of the aims of this book is to impress on our minds the fact that Jesus Christ is the most important person in the universe. Not more (or less) important than God the Father or God the Spirit, of course. With them, he is equal in worth and beauty and wisdom and justice and love and power. But he is more important than all created persons—whether angels or demons or kings or commanders or scientists or artists or philosophers or athletes or musicians or actors—the ones who live now, or have ever lived, or ever will live. Jesus Christ is supreme.

ALL THINGS *FOR* JESUS—EVEN EVIL

This book is also meant to show that everything that exists—including evil—is ordained by an infinitely holy and all-wise God to make the glory of Christ shine more brightly. The word *ordained* is peculiar, I know. But I want to be clear what I mean by it. There is no attempt to obscure what I am saying about God's relation to evil. But there *is* an attempt to say carefully what the Bible says. By *ordain* I mean that God either *caused* something directly or *permitted* it for wise purposes. This permitting is a kind of *indirect* causing, since God knows all the factors involved and what effects they will have and he could prevent any outcome. So his *permission* is a kind of secondary causing, but not a direct causing.[1] This distinction is an effort to be faithful to the different ways the Bible speaks about God's relation to events.

---

[1]I find the effort of Stephen Charnock (1628–1680), a chaplain to Henry Cromwell and a non-conformist pastor in London, to be balanced and helpful in holding the diverse Scriptures on God's will together. He writes:

> God doth not will [sin] directly, and by an efficacious will. He doth not directly will it, because he hath prohibited it by his law, which is a discovery of his will; so that if he should directly will sin, and directly prohibit it, he would will good and evil in the same manner, and there would be contradictions in God's will: to will sin absolutely, is to work it (Psalm 115:3): "God hath done whatsoever he pleased." God cannot absolutely will it, because he cannot work it. God wills good by a positive decree, because he hath decreed to effect it. He wills evil by a private decree, because he hath decreed not to give that grace which would certainly prevent it. God doth not will sin simply, for that were to approve it, but he wills it, in order to that good his wisdom will bring forth from it. He wills not sin for itself, but for the event. (Stephen Charnock, *Discourses upon the Existence and Attributes of God* [Grand Rapids, MI: Baker Book House, 1979], 148.)

Some people disparage an appeal to "secondary causes" between God's sovereign will and the immediate effecting of a sinful act (cf. Jack Cottrell, "The Nature of the Divine Sovereignty," *The Grace of God and the Will of Man* [Minneapolis: Bethany House, 1995], 100–102). But this idea of intermediate causes, which is different from God's ultimate causing, is not introduced because of the demands of a theological system, but because so many Scriptures demand it. For example, 1) God commissions an "evil spirit" between Abimelech and the men of Shechem to bring about his will (Judg. 9:22–24); 2) in Luke 22:3 Satan leads Judas to do what Acts 2:23 says God brought about; 3) Paul says that Satan blinds the minds of unbelievers (2 Cor. 4:4), but also says that God sends a blinding spirit of stupor (Rom. 11:8–10); 4) Satan stirs up David to take a census (1 Chron. 21:1), which proved

The Bible expresses both ideas—causing and permitting—in the way God brings things about. For example, in Mark 5:12–13, the demons beg to be sent into the pigs, and Jesus "gave them *permission.*" In 1 Corinthians 16:7 Paul says, "I hope to spend some time with you, if the Lord *permits.*" Hebrews 6:1–3 exhorts the people to "leave elementary doctrine . . . and go on to maturity," then concludes, "And this we will do if God *permits.*"

And the Bible speaks of God's more direct action even in events that involve evil. For example, Joseph's brothers sold him into slavery. By this sinful act Joseph goes to Egypt and later is in a position to save the very brothers who hated him. Joseph says, "God *sent* me before you to preserve for you a remnant on earth" (Gen. 45:7).

At the exodus from Egypt, we read about God's hardening the heart of Pharaoh and his turning the Egyptians to hate the Israelites. "I will harden his heart, so that he will not let the people go" (Ex. 4:21). "He turned their hearts to hate his people, to deal craftily with his servants" (Ps. 105:25).

And when it comes to calamities—physical and spiritual—they are repeatedly described as sent by God. "I will send famine and wild beasts against you, and they will rob you of your children" (Ezek. 5:17). "I will send a famine on the land—not a famine of bread, nor a thirst for water, but of hearing the words of the LORD" (Amos 8:11).

---

to be sin (2 Sam. 24:10), and yet it is written that God was in some sense the cause behind Satan (2 Sam. 24:1); 5) Satan gets permission from God to torment Job (Job 1:12; 2:6), but when Satan had taken Job's family and made him sick, Job said, "The Lord has taken away" (Job 1:21), and, "Shall we receive good from God and shall we not receive evil" (2:10)—to which the writer responds: "In all this Job did not sin with his lips" (1:22; 2:10). Texts like these make the theological reflections of Theodore Beza (in 1582) biblically sound:

> Nothing happens anyhow or without God's most righteous decree, although God is not the author of or sharer in any sin at all. Both His power and His goodness are so great and so incomprehensible, that at a time when He applies the devil or wicked men in achieving some work, whom He afterwards justly punishes, He Himself none the less effects His holy work well and justly. These things do not hinder but rather establish second and intermediate causes, by which all things happen. When from eternity God decreed whatever was to happen at definite moments, He at the same time also decreed the manner and way which He wished it thus to take place; to such extent, that even if some flaw is discovered in a second cause, it yet implies no flaw or fault in God's eternal counsel. (Quoted in Heinrich Heppe, *Reformed Dogmatics* [Grand Rapids, MI: Baker Book House, 1978, orig. 1860], 143–144.)

So when I say that everything that exists—including evil—is *ordained* by an infinitely holy and all-wise God to make the glory of Christ shine more brightly, I mean that, one way or the other, God sees to it that all things serve to glorify his Son. Whether he causes or permits, he does so with purpose. For an infinitely wise and all-knowing God, both causing and permitting are purposeful. They are part of the big picture of what God plans to bring to pass.

EVIL EXISTS FOR ITS APPOINTED PURPOSE

The Bible is explicit that wickedness exists for God's wise purposes. For example, Proverbs 16:4 says, "The LORD has made everything for its purpose, even the wicked for the day of trouble." God has done this in his own mysterious way that preserves the responsibility of the wicked and the sinlessness of his own heart. We should humble ourselves if we cannot explain how this can be. We are told that it is so. Beware of bringing to the Bible assumptions that are not taught in the Bible. That is how God's word is nullified.

We saw in Chapter Two that all things were made through Christ and *for* Christ (Col. 1:16). We saw that this explicitly includes the "thrones or dominions or rulers or authorities" that were defeated by Christ at the cross. In other words, they were made "for the day of trouble," as Proverbs 16:4 implies. God knew what they would become when he created them, and he folded their evil into his plan of redemption. On Good Friday, when Christ died and the evil powers were defeated, the power and justice and wrath and love of Christ were displayed. Sooner or later every rebellion against him comes to ruin and serves to glorify Christ.

THE GOD WHO IS THERE

This book also aims to solidify the conviction that Christianity is not merely a set of ideas and practices and feelings designed for our psychological well-being—whether designed by God or man. That's not what Christianity is. Christianity begins with the conviction that God is an objective reality outside ourselves. We do not make him what he is by thinking a certain way about him. As Francis Schaeffer said, he is *the God who is there*. We don't make him. He makes us. We don't decide what he is going to be like. He decides what we are going to be like. He created the universe, and it has the meaning he gives it, not the meaning *we* give it. If we give it a meaning different from his, we are fools. And our lives will be tragic in the end.

Christianity is not a game; it's not a therapy. All of its doctrines flow from who God is and what he has done in history. They correspond to hard facts. Christianity is more than facts, but not less. There is faith and hope and love. But these don't float in the air. They grow like great cedar trees in the rock of God's truth.

And the reason I make this one of my aims in this book is because I am deeply convinced from the Bible that our eternal joy and strength and holiness depend on the solidity of this worldview putting strong fiber into the spine of our faith. Wimpy worldviews make wimpy Christians. And wimpy Christians won't survive the days ahead. Rootless emotionalism that treats Christianity like a therapeutic option will be swept away in the last days. Those who will be left standing will be those who have built their houses on the rock of great, objective truth with Jesus Christ as the origin, center, and goal of it all.

JESUS' GLORY PLANNED IN ADAM'S SIN

The focus of this chapter is on the spectacular sin of the first man, Adam, and how it set the stage for the more spectacular counter-thrust of Jesus Christ. We turn now to Romans 5:12–21.[2]

The glory of Christ is the main purpose that God had in

---

[2]When I preached through Romans at Bethlehem Baptist Church, I devoted five sermons to these verses. Those sermons are at www.desiringGod.org. In this chapter, the focus is different from anything I looked at in those messages.

mind when he permitted Adam's sin, and with it the Fall of all humanity into sin. Remember what we have seen about God's permission: Whatever God permits, he permits for a reason. And his reasons are always infinitely wise and purposeful. He did not have to let the Fall of Satan or of Adam happen. He could have stopped it.

The fact that he did not stop it means he has a reason, a purpose for it. And he doesn't make up his plans as he goes along. What he knows to be wise, he has always known to be wise—eternally. Therefore, Adam's sin and the Fall of the human race with him into sin and misery did not take God off guard. It is part of God's overarching plan with the aim of it all to display the fullness of the glory of Jesus Christ.

One of the clearest ways to show this from the Bible—and we won't go into it in detail here[3]—is to look at those places where the sin-defeating sacrifice of Christ is shown to be in God's mind before the creation of the world.

For example, in Revelation 13:8, John writes about "everyone whose name has not been written *before the foundation of the world* in the book of life of the Lamb who was slain." So there was a book before the foundation of the world called "the book of life of the Lamb who was slain." Before the world was created, God had already planned that his Son would be slain like a lamb to save all those who are written in the book.

Or consider 2 Timothy 1:9: "[God] saved us and called us to a holy calling, not because of our works but because of his own purpose and *grace, which he gave us in Christ Jesus before the ages began.*" Saving grace was given to us before the ages began. That is, it was given to us before there was any human sin to save us from. Therefore, grace was planned before human sin was there to need it. This means that God's plan to save us through grace was not a response to human

---

[3]For a fuller development of this, see my chapter "Why God Appoints Suffering for His Servants" in *Suffering and the Sovereignty of Christ*, ed. John Piper and Justin Taylor (Wheaton, IL.: Crossway Books, 2006), 91–109.

decisions to sin. Saving grace was the plan that made sin necessary. God did not find sin in the world and then make a plan to remedy it. He had the plan before the ages, and that plan was for the glory of sin-conquering grace through the death of Jesus Christ.

This is even more plain in Ephesians 1:4–6: "[God] chose us in [Christ] before the foundation of the world, that we should be holy and blameless before him. In love he predestined us for adoption as sons through Jesus Christ, according to the purpose of his will, to the praise of his glorious grace, with which he has blessed us in the Beloved." To what end did God predestine us sinners for adoption? To the praise of the glory of his grace. That is why the plan was made. The ultimate aim of the eternal plan was that praise might be as intense as possible for the glory of God's grace. And the apex of that glory is in the death of Jesus. So much so that the gospel of the death of Christ for sinners is called "the gospel of *the glory of Christ*, who is the image of God" (2 Cor. 4:4).

Therefore, the biblical view is that the sufferings and death of Christ for sin are not planned after the actual sin of Adam but before. Therefore, when the sin of Adam happens, God is not surprised by it, but has already made it part of his plan—namely, a plan to display his amazing patience and grace and justice and wrath in the history of redemption, and then, climactically, to reveal the greatness of his Son as the second Adam superior in every way to the first Adam.

So we look at Romans 5:12–21, keeping in mind that Adam's spectacular sin did not frustrate God's Christ-exalting purposes, but instead served them. Here's the way we will look at these verses. There are five explicit references to Christ. One of them sets up the way Paul is thinking about Christ and Adam. And the other four show how Christ is greater than Adam. Two of those four are so similar we will lump them together. Which means we will look at three aspects of Christ's superiority.

JESUS, "THE COMING ONE"

Notice the way Christ is referred to in verse 14. Verses 12–13 supply the context: "Therefore, just as sin came into the world through one man, and death through sin, and so death spread to all men because all sinned—for sin indeed was in the world before the law was given, but sin is not counted where there is no law. Yet death reigned from Adam to Moses, even over those whose sinning was not like the transgression of Adam, who was a type of the one who was to come." There's the reference to Christ in verse 14: "the one who was to come."

This verse sets up the way Paul is thinking in the rest of the passage. Notice the most obvious thing first: Christ "was to come." From the beginning, Christ was "the coming one." Paul shows that Christ is not an afterthought. Paul does not say that Christ was conceived as a copy of Adam. He says that Adam was a type of Christ. God dealt with Adam in a way that would make him a type of the way he planned to glorify his Son. A type is a foreshadowing of something that will come later and will be like the type—only greater. So God dealt with Adam in a way that would make him a type of Christ. God's plan for Christ preceded his dealing with Adam.

Notice more closely just where, in the flow of his thought, Paul chooses to say that Adam is a type of Christ. Verse 14: "Yet death reigned from Adam to Moses, even over those whose sinning was not like the transgression of Adam, *who was a type of the one who was to come.*" He chooses to tell us that Adam is a type of Christ just after saying that even people who did not sin in the way Adam did still bore the punishment that Adam bore. Why did Paul, just at this point, say that Adam was a type of Christ?

JESUS, OUR REPRESENTATIVE HEAD

What he had just said gets at the very essence of how Christ and Adam are *alike* and the way they are *different.* Here's the parallel: People whose transgression was not like Adam's died like Adam. Why? Because they were connected to Adam. He was the representative head of their humanity, and his sin is counted as their sin because of their connection with him. That's the essence of why Adam is called a type of Christ—because our obedience is not like Christ's obedience and yet we have eternal life with Christ. Why? Because we are connected to Christ by faith. He is the representative head of the new humanity, and his righteousness is counted as our righteousness because of our connection with him (Rom. 6:5).

That's the parallel implied in calling Adam a type of Christ:

Adam	>Adam's sin	>humanity condemned in him	>eternal death
Christ	>Christ's righteousness	>new humanity justified in him	>eternal life

The rest of the passage unpacks how much greater Christ and his saving work are than Adam and his destructive work. Keep in mind what I said at the beginning of this chapter. What we are seeing here is God's revelation of realities that define the world that every person on this planet lives in. Everybody on this planet is included in this text because Adam was the father of everybody. Therefore, every person you meet, of any ethnicity, is facing what this text talks about. Death in Adam or life in Christ.

This is a global text. Don't miss that. This is the defining reality for every single person you will ever meet. Wimpy worldviews produce wimpy Christians. This is not a wimpy worldview. It stretches over all of history and over all the earth. It profoundly affects every person in the world and every headline on the Internet.

CELEBRATING THE SUPERIORITY OF JESUS

Now let's look at three ways that Paul celebrates how Christ and his work are superior over Adam and his work. They can be summed up under three phrases: (1) the abundance of grace, (2) the perfection of obedience, and (3) the reign of life.

The Abounding Grace of Christ

First, verse 15 and the abundance of grace. "But the free gift [of righteousness, v. 17] is not like the trespass. For if many died through one man's trespass, much more have the grace of God and the free gift by the grace of that one man Jesus Christ abounded for many." The point here is that God's grace is more powerful than Adam's trespass. That's what the words *much more* signify: "much more has the grace of God . . . abounded for many." If man's trespass brought death, how much more will God's grace bring life.

But Paul is more specific than that. God's grace is specifically "the grace of that one man Jesus Christ." "Much more have the grace of God and the free gift by *the grace of that one man Jesus Christ* abounded for many." These are not two different graces. "The grace of that one man Jesus Christ" is the incarnation of the grace of God. That's the way Paul talks about it, for example, in Titus 2:11: "The grace of God has appeared [namely, in Jesus], bringing salvation. . . ." And in 2 Timothy 1:9: "his own . . . grace, which he gave us in Christ Jesus." So the grace that is in Jesus is the grace of God.

This grace is sovereign grace. It conquers everything in its path. We will see in just a moment that it has the power of the king of the universe. It is reigning grace. That's the first celebration of Christ's superiority over Adam. When the trespass of the one man Adam and the grace of the one man Jesus Christ meet, Adam and his trespass lose. Christ and his grace win. That is very good news for those who belong to Christ.

The Perfect Obedience of Christ

Second, Paul celebrates the way that the grace of Christ conquers Adam's trespass and death, namely, the perfection of Christ's obedience. Verse 19: "For as by the one man's disobedience [namely, Adam's] the many were made sinners, so by the one man's obedience [namely, Christ's] the many will be made righteous." So the grace of the one man, Jesus Christ, keeps him from sinning—keeps him obedient unto death, even death on the cross (Phil. 2:8)—so that he offers flawless and complete obedience to the Father on behalf of those who are connected to him by faith. Adam failed in his obedience. Christ succeeded perfectly. Adam was the source of sin and death. Christ was the source of obedience and life.

Christ is like Adam, who was a type of Christ—both are the representative heads of an old and a new humanity. God imputes the failure of Adam to his humanity, and God imputes the success of Christ to his humanity, because of how these two humanities are united to their respective heads. The great superiority of Christ is that he not only succeeds in obeying perfectly, but does so in such a way that millions of people are counted righteous because of his obedience. Are you only connected to Adam? Are you only a part of the first humanity bound for death? Or are you also connected to Christ and part of the new humanity bound for eternal life?

The Reign of Life

Third, Paul celebrates not only the abounding grace of Christ and the perfect obedience of Christ, but finally, the reign of life through Christ. Grace leads through Christ's obedience to the triumph of eternal life. Verse 21: ". . . so that, as sin reigned in death, grace also might reign through righteousness leading to eternal life through Jesus Christ our Lord." Grace reigns through righteousness (that is, through the perfect righteousness of Christ) to the great climax of eternal life—and all of that is "through Jesus Christ our Lord."

Or, once more in verse 17, the same point: "For if, because of one man's trespass, death reigned through that one man, much more will those who receive the abundance of grace and the free gift of righteousness reign in life through the one man Jesus Christ." The same pattern: Grace through the free gift of righteousness leads to the triumph of life, and all of that through Jesus Christ.

I mentioned above that the grace of God in Christ that Paul

refers to in these verses is sovereign grace. You can see that in the word *reign*. Death has a kind of sovereignty over man and reigns over all. All die. But grace conquers sin and death. It reigns in life even over those who once were dead. That is sovereign grace.

JESUS' SPECTACULAR OBEDIENCE

This is the great glory of Christ—he vastly outshines the first man Adam. The spectacular sin of Adam is not as great as the spectacular grace and obedience of Christ and the gift of eternal life. Indeed, God's plan from the beginning, in his perfect righteousness, was that Adam, as the representative head of humankind, would be a type of Christ as the representative head of a new humanity. His plan was that by this comparison and contrast, the glory of Christ would shine all the more brightly.

Verse 17 puts the matter to us very personally and very urgently. Where do we stand? "For if, because of one man's trespass, death reigned through that one man, much more will *those who receive the abundance of grace and the free gift of righteousness* reign in life through the one man Jesus Christ." Read these words very carefully and personally: "those who *receive* the abundance of grace and the free gift of righteousness."

PRECIOUS WORDS FOR SINNERS

These are precious words for sinners like you and me: The grace is free, the gift is free, the righteousness of Christ is free. The question is: Will we receive it as the hope and treasure of our lives? If we do, we will "reign in life through the one man Jesus Christ." And in this eternal reign, we will enjoy as our supreme Treasure the beauty and worth of Jesus Christ whose glory shines all the more brightly against the backdrop of Adam's spectacular sin. The point of Romans 5:12–21 is that Christ's saving achievement is understood and cherished as it should be in view of Adam's spectacular sin. This was not a coincidence. It was God's purpose before the foundation of the world.

5

THE PRIDE OF BABEL
AND THE PRAISE
OF CHRIST

How the Judgment of God Brings
Joyful Acclaim to Jesus

"Come, let us build ourselves a city and a tower with its top in the heavens, and let us make a name for ourselves."
GENESIS 11:4

So the LORD dispersed them from there over the face of all the earth, and they left off building the city. Therefore its name was called Babel, because there the LORD confused the language of all the earth.
GENESIS 11:8–9

Our theme in this book is *Spectacular Sins and Their Global Purpose in the Glory of Christ*. In this chapter, we come to the spectacular sin of the building of the tower of Babel. Lest you think this is too distant and irrelevant to your modern life, ask these questions: Where do all the languages in the world come from—and all the people groups? Are they the result of sin? Are they a good idea, full of potential for the glory of Christ and the joy of God's people? Is it good or bad that there are separate, independent political states that are often in conflict? What does God think of a monolithic super-state? Will he prevent one? Will the world end with one? And personally, what is your own root sin, and what does God think of it? What has he done to rescue you from it? All of that and more flows out of this account.

A PERPLEXING MATTER ANSWERED

Let's begin by clarifying one perplexing matter of context. Genesis 11:1–9 seems to describe the origin of languages. But careful readers of Genesis notice that in chapter 10 the peoples and languages are described *already*, before the tower of Babel in Genesis 11.

For example, look at Genesis 10:5: "The coastland peoples spread in their lands, each with his own language, by their clans, in their nations." Then you get to Genesis 11:1 which says, "Now the whole earth had one language and the same words." The author knew what he was doing. He has not forgotten in 11:1 what he had just written in 10:5, 20, and 31 (only two verses earlier).

The solution is to recognize that the author has not put these two stories in chronological order. He first describes the spread of the peoples and languages in chapter 10, and then he describes the origin of that diversity in 11:1–9. Sometimes, when you have something shocking to say about why an event happens, you put it at the beginning of the event, and sometimes you wait and put it at the end of the event.

After the Flood, God had said to Noah in Genesis 9:1, "Be fruitful and multiply and fill the earth." That's what chapter 10 describes. It was happening as peoples and languages multiplied. It looked like a simple fulfillment of God's command. It looked like obedience. Then Genesis 11:1–9 drops the bomb on us. It wasn't obedience after all. The people weren't spreading to fill the earth. They were clustering. God came down and shattered their disobedience and made their clustering impossible. He confused their language and broke humanity into many peoples and languages.

TWO GREAT SINS EXPOSED

Let's dig in here for a moment and see what the sin was and then what God's judgment was before we ask how all this is designed for the glory of Christ. Genesis 11:1–4 reads,

> Now the whole earth had one language and the same words. And as people migrated from the east, they found a plain in the land of Shinar and settled there. And they said to one another, "Come, let us make bricks, and burn them thoroughly." And they had brick for stone, and bitumen for mortar. Then they said, "Come, let us build ourselves a city and a tower with its top in the heavens, and let us make a name for ourselves, lest we be dispersed over the face of the whole earth."

The key statements are in verse 4: (1) They aim to build a city. (2) They aim to build a tower in the city that reaches to the heavens. (3) They aim to make a name for themselves. (4) They aim not to be dispersed over the whole earth. The first two of these correspond to the second two.

Building a city is the way one avoids being dispersed over the whole earth. And building a tower into the heavens is the way one makes a name for oneself. So the city and tower are the outward expressions of the inward sins. The two sins are the love of praise (so you crave to make a name for yourself) and the love of security (so you build a city and don't take the risks of filling the earth).

God's will for human beings is not that we find our joy in being praised, but that we find our joy in knowing and praising him. His will is not that we find our security in cities but in God whom we gladly obey. So the spectacular sin of man is that even after the Flood, which was a thunderclap of warning against sin for Noah and his descendants, it turns out that we are no better now than we were before the Flood. The human condition is just like it was with Adam and Eve. We will decide for ourselves what is best. We think we can even rise up and claim the place of God. This is the story of mankind to this very day apart from redeeming grace.

ADAM'S SIN REPLAYED

Two things in verse 5 signal that man is about to be put in his place. "The LORD came down to see the city and the tower, which the children of man had built." First, notice that he calls them "the children of man," or translated another way, "the sons of Adam." The building of this city and this tower are similar to what Adam did when he rebelled against God and ate of the tree. The sinful nature of Adam goes on in his descendants—including you and me.

HOLY SCORN DISPLAYED

Second, notice that it says, "The Lord *came down* to see the city and the tower." This is holy scorn. The author mocks the tower by saying that God had to *come down* to see it. This tower is so far from being in heaven, God can't see it from heaven! Of course, God can see everything everywhere. But when you want to show the ludicrous nature of man's God-belittling pride in his little achievements, you take some risks, and you speak with irony and you describe God as peering down in search of this great tower "with its top in the heavens."

GLOBAL ASPIRATIONS LIMITED

Now what will God do in response to this spectacular sin of man who is refusing to fill the earth with God's glory, instead securing his life in a city, and trying to exalt himself to the place of God? Genesis 11:6–8 says:

> And the LORD said, "Behold, they are one people, and they
> have all one language, and this is only the beginning of what
> they will do. And nothing that they propose to do will now be
> impossible for them. Come, let us go down and there confuse

their language, so that they may not understand one another's speech." So the LORD dispersed them from there over the face of all the earth, and they left off building the city.

Notice what God says in verse 6: "Behold, they are one people, and they have all one language." That signals that God is not only about to divide their language, but in doing so is about to divide one people into many peoples. He is about to multiply languages and peoples. So God says in verse 7, "Come, let us go down and there confuse their language, so that they may not understand one another's speech." In this way, God dispersed them over the face of all the earth.

So his response to the presumption and arrogance of man was to make it harder for man to communicate and thus harder to unite in God-belittling global plans. God has built into the world a system by which the pride of different groups of people restrains the pride of other groups of people. God knows the immense potential of human beings created in his own image. And he has given them amazing liberty to exalt themselves and design their own security systems without trusting him. But there are limits. Thousands of languages around the world and thousands of different peoples limit the global aspirations of arrogant mankind.

HOW WAS THIS DESIGNED TO GLORIFY CHRIST?

Now turn with me to the question of God's global design in all this for the glory of Christ. Keep in mind the principle we have leaned on repeatedly: *When God permits something, he does so for a reason.* And that reason is part of a plan. God does not act whimsically or haphazardly or aimlessly. So when he permits this spectacular sin of the pride and presumption and rebellion on the plains of Shinar, he knows exactly what he is doing and what his response to it will be. Which means that the peoples and languages of the world are not an afterthought. They are the judgment of God on sin, and at the same time, they are designed by God for the global glory of Jesus Christ.

So we ask again: How does this spectacular sin and its consequence in the divided languages of the world serve to magnify the glory of Christ? Here are five ways.

Christians Guarded

God's division of the world into different languages hinders the rise of a global, monolithic anti-Christian state that would have the power to simply wipe out all Christians. We often think that the diversity of languages and cultures and peoples and political states is a hindrance to world evangelization—the spread of Christ's glory. That's not the way God sees it. God is more concerned about the dangers of human uniformity than he is about human diversity. We humans are far too evil to be allowed to unite in one language or one government. The gospel of the glory of Christ spreads better and flourishes more *because* of 6,500 languages, not in spite of them.

Pride Destroyed

Here is a second way that the story of the tower of Babel glorifies Christ. Suppose someone asks, "But isn't there going to be in the last days a great global government and won't Christians in fact be persecuted everywhere?" The answer is yes. In the last days, God will loosen the restraints that now hold back this evil. The Antichrist—"the man of lawlessness" as Paul calls him (2 Thess. 2:3), "the beast" as John calls him (Rev. 13:3)—will rise with great global attraction, and there will be horrific persecution of Christians. But here's the link with the rebels of Shinar. The tower they built was called the tower of *Babel* (Gen. 11:9).

The word *babel* in Hebrew occurs over two hundred times in the Old Testament and is translated *Babylon* in all but a few. When the writer says in Genesis 11:9, "Therefore its name was called Babel [*babel*], because there the LORD confused the language of all the earth," it's a putdown of the great city of Babylon. It means that Babylon, with its vaunted towers and walls and gardens and idolatry, is a pitiful effort compared to God. And this name *Babel* or *Babylon* is the name given to the city of the Beast in the book of Revelation (14:8–9). And in this, the glory of Christ shines because, even though for a brief season Babylon is drunk with the blood of Christian martyrs (Rev. 17:6), she will, just like the tower of Babel, be brought to naught. Here's a description that marks her out as a latter-day "tower of Babel."

> Her sins are heaped high as heaven. . . . As she glorified herself and lived in luxury, so give her a like measure of torment and mourning, since in her heart she says, "I sit as a queen, I am no widow, and mourning I shall never see." . . . "Alas! Alas! You great city, you mighty city, Babylon! For in a single hour your judgment has come." (Rev. 18:5, 7, 10)

So, yes, in the last days God will loosen the restraint he has put on the nations. They will swell with the pride of Babylon. Christians will suffer. And then, in one instant, Christ will come from his infinite heights and slay the man of lawlessness with the breath of his mouth (2 Thess. 2:8). And Babylon will be no more. The pride of man will be eliminated from the earth. The story of Genesis 11:1–9 is a foreshadowing of that. The victory there and at the end is the victory of Christ.

Every Group Claimed

Here is a third way that the sin of Babel and God's judgment on it leads to the global glory of Christ. The authority and power of Jesus is magnified because he lays claim on every language group and every people. "All authority in heaven and on earth has been given to me. Go therefore and make disciples of all nations" (Matt. 28:18–19). Yes, in response to sin, God has divided the languages and the nations. But in the end, it magnifies the authority and power of Christ to make disciples in every language. His power is all the more glorious because it breaks into so many different languages and peoples and brings salvation.[1]

The Gospel Glorified

And the same must be said about the gospel of Christ in particular—the message of his death and resurrection, the message of forgiveness and justification. Romans 1:16: "I am not ashamed of the gospel, for it is the power of God for salvation to everyone who believes, *to the Jew first and also to the Greek.*" A great part of the glory of the gospel is that it is not provincial. It is not a tribal religion. It breaks into every language and every people. If there were no diversity of languages, if the spectacular sin of Babel had not happened with its judgment, the global glory of the gospel of Christ would not shine as beautifully as it does in the prism of thousands of languages.

Jesus Praised

And finally, the praise that Jesus receives from all the languages of the world is more beautiful because of its diversity than it would have been if there were only one language and one people to sing. "And they sang a new song, saying, 'Worthy are you to take the scroll and to open its seals, for you were slain, and by your blood you ransomed people for God *from every tribe and language and people and nation,* and you have made them a kingdom and priests to our God, and they shall reign on the earth" (Rev. 5:9–10). "After this I looked, and behold, a great multitude that no one could number, *from every nation, from all tribes and peoples and languages,* standing before the throne and before the Lamb, clothed in white robes, with palm branches in their hands, and crying out with a loud voice, 'Salvation belongs to our God who sits on the throne, and to the Lamb!'" (Rev. 7:9–10).

It was the spectacular sin on the plains of Shinar that gave

---

[1]See a fuller explanation of how the diversity of cultures glorifies Christ in John Piper, *Let the Nations Be Glad,* second edition (Grand Rapids, MI.: Baker, 2003), 196–200.

rise to the multiplying of languages that ends in the most glorious praise to Christ from every language on earth. Therefore, from every language and people, praise the Lord! Let everything that has breath praise the Lord!

6

THE SALE OF JOSEPH
AND THE SON OF GOD

How Salvation Comes through Slavery

"And God sent me before you to preserve for you a remnant on earth, and to keep alive for you many survivors."

GENESIS 45:7

"As for you, you meant evil against me, but God meant it for good, to bring it about that many people should be kept alive, as they are today."

GENESIS 50:20

"The scepter shall not depart from Judah, nor the ruler's staff from between his feet, until tribute comes to him; and to him shall be the obedience of the peoples."

GENESIS 49:10

The story of Joseph's fall and rise through the sins of his brothers and the sovereignty of God is overflowing with lessons about the ways of God and the (seeming!) detours of our lives. One of the most famous sayings of the Bible is in this story. It has shed painfully comforting light on a thousand tragedies: You meant it for evil, but God meant it for good. The "you" in that sentence could be anyone who does something that hurts you, even the devil himself. What we will see is that this story points finally to the One who was hurt worse than anyone by his enemies, and in that very abuse and pain God meant it for good—infinite good.

THE COVENANT PEOPLE, ISRAEL

Before we look at the last chapters of Genesis and retell the story of Joseph and the spectacular sin of his brothers and its global purpose in the glory of Jesus Christ, let's back up to Genesis 12. God has chosen Abram from all the peoples of the world by free grace and owing to nothing in him. In Genesis 12:2–3, God makes him a promise: "I will bless you and make your name great, so that you will be a blessing. I will bless those who bless you, and him who dishonors you I will curse, and in you all the families of the earth shall be blessed." This is the beginning of the people of Israel through whom Jesus Christ, the Messiah, the Son of God. would come into the world to save us from our sins.

FOUR HUNDRED YEARS!

Then in Genesis 15, God makes a formal covenant with Abram. He uses a remarkable symbolic act and some astonishing words. He says to Abram in Genesis 15:13–16,

> Know for certain that your offspring will be sojourners in a land that is not theirs and will be servants there, and they will be afflicted for four hundred years. But I will bring judgment on the nation that they serve, and afterward they shall come out with great possessions. . . . And they shall come back here in the fourth generation, for the iniquity of the Amorites is not yet complete.

So at the very beginning of his covenant relationship with his chosen people, God predicts a four-hundred-year stay in Egypt and then a return to the Promised Land. "They will be afflicted four hundred years." He has his strange reasons why they must leave for four centuries (Think of it! Four centuries!) and not inherit the land now, namely (verse 15), "The iniquity of the Amorites is not yet complete."

When the Israelites come back to take the land under Joshua in four hundred years, they will destroy these nations at God's command. How are we to understand that? Deuteronomy 9:5 gives God's answer: "Not because of your righteousness or the uprightness of your heart are you going in to possess their land, but because of the wickedness of these nations the LORD your God is driving them out from before you, and that he may confirm the word that the LORD swore to your fathers, to Abraham, to Isaac, and to Jacob." The conquest of the Promised Land is the judgment of God on the fullness of centuries of wickedness.

GOD'S PEOPLE ENTER THROUGH MANY AFFLICTIONS

In the meantime, God says that his people will be sojourners in a land that is not theirs, namely, in Egypt, and will be afflicted for four hundred years. So there is God's plan for his pilgrim people—a kind of picture of our life on this earth until heaven. If God plans four hundred years of affliction for his people (Gen. 15:13) before the Promised Land, we should not be surprised that he says to us, "through many tribulations you must enter the kingdom of God" (Acts 14:22).

PROPHECY FULFILLED THROUGH A SPECTACULAR SIN

The question for us is: How will it come about that God's people wind up in Egypt? And what does God want to teach about his ways and about his Son in this strange sojourn in Egypt? The answer is that God fulfills this prophecy through a spectacular sin. And through this sin, he preserves alive not only his covenant people of Israel, but also the line from which the Lion of Judah would come to save and rule the peoples. Huge things are at stake in the story of Joseph.

DESTROYING THE DREAMER

Going back to Abram, let's bring the story up to Joseph. Abram has a son Isaac. Isaac has a son Jacob (whose other name is Israel), and Jacob has twelve sons who become the fathers of the twelve tribes of Israel. One of Jacob's twelve sons, Joseph, has two dreams. In both of them, his eleven brothers and his parents bow down to him. Genesis 37:8 says that his brothers hated him for these dreams. And verse 11 says they were jealous.

The day finally comes when they can vent their rage against their brother. His father sends him to see if it is well with his brothers (Genesis 37:14). They see him coming and say in verses 19–20, "Here comes this dreamer. Come now, let us kill him and throw him into one of the pits. Then we will say that a fierce animal has devoured him, and we will see what will become of his dreams." Reuben tries to save Joseph, but his attempt is only partly successful when the brothers sell Joseph as a slave to a caravan of Ishmaelites heading for Egypt (Gen. 37:27–28). They keep his special coat and soak it in animal blood, and his father assumes he was eaten by wild animals. The brothers think that is the end of the matter.

AN INVISIBLE HAND AT WORK

But they have no idea what is happening. They are utterly oblivious to God's invisible hand in their action. They do not know that in the very effort to destroy this dreamer, they are fulfilling Joseph's dreams. Oh, how often God works this way! He takes the very sins of the destroyers and makes them the means of the destroyers' deliverance.

POTIPHAR, PRISON, AND PROVIDENCE

In Egypt, Joseph is purchased by Potiphar, an officer of Pharaoh and captain of the guard (Gen. 37:36). Joseph submits to God's strange providence and serves Potiphar faithfully. He rises with trust and influence over Potiphar's household. And you would think that the righteous would prosper. But it seems to be otherwise. Potiphar's wife tries to seduce Joseph. He flees fornication. And the spurned woman is vicious and lies about Joseph. In spite of his righteousness, he is put in prison.

In prison, again, totally unaware of what God is doing in all this misery, he serves the jailer faithfully and is given trust and responsibility. Through the interpretation of two dreams of Pharaoh's butler and baker, Joseph is eventually brought out of prison to interpret one of Pharaoh's dreams. His interpretation proves true, and his wisdom seems compelling to Pharaoh. So Joseph is made commander in Egypt. "You shall be over my house," Pharaoh says, "and all my people shall order themselves as you command. Only as regards the throne will I be greater than you" (Gen. 41:40).

THE DREAMS FULFILLED

Seven years of plenty followed by seven years of famine strike the land, just as Joseph said they would. Joseph preempts starvation in Egypt by gathering huge reserves of grain during the seven good years. Eventually Joseph's brothers hear that there is grain in Egypt, and they go for help.

They don't recognize their brother at first, but eventually he reveals himself. He had been seventeen years old when they sold him into slavery (37:2). Now when he identifies himself, he is thirty-nine years old (41:46, 53; 45:6). Twenty-two years had gone by. They are stunned. They tried to get rid of the dreamer, and in getting rid of him, they fulfilled his dreams. The brothers are bowing down at last to Joseph just as the dreams said they would.

Eventually, he invites them to live in Egypt to save their

lives. The fulfillment of the distant prophecy that Abraham's seed would sojourn four hundred years in Egypt begins. So we ask again: How did it come about that God's people wind up in Egypt in fulfillment of God's plan? And what does God want to teach us about his ways and about his Son in this strange sojourn in Egypt?

TWO BIBLICAL DESCRIPTIONS OF THIS FULFILLMENT

The answer to how the people wound up in Egypt is clear at one level: They got there by means of the spectacular sin of attempted murder, greedy slave-dealing, and the heartless deceiving of a brokenhearted old man. But how does the Bible describe this fulfillment of God's prophecy? In two ways.

God Sent Joseph to Preserve Life

First, in Genesis 45:5, Joseph says to his brothers who are very afraid of him, "Do not be distressed or angry with yourselves because you sold me here, for *God sent me before you* to preserve life." The first way the Bible describes this spectacular sin of the brothers is that it was God's way of sending Joseph to Egypt in order to save the very ones who were trying to kill him. "God sent me before you."

And lest we think this was a side comment with little significance, we read the very same thing in Psalm 105:16–17—only there the stakes are raised even higher. Not only was God ruling the actions of these brothers to get Joseph to Egypt, but God was ruling the famine as well: "When he summoned a famine on the land and broke all supply of bread, he had sent a man ahead of them, Joseph, who was sold as a slave." So we should put out of our minds the thought that God simply *foresaw* a famine happening on its own, or happening by Satan. God summoned the famine. And God prepared the deliverance. And he did it through a spectacular sin.

What Man Designed for Evil, God Designed for Good

So the first way the Bible describes the fulfillment of God's prophecy that his people would come to Egypt is by saying *God sent Joseph* there ahead of them. The second way the Bible describes this prophecy is even more penetrating and sweeping. The brothers come before Joseph again, this time after the death of their father, and they are again afraid he will take vengeance on them. In Genesis 50:19–20, Joseph says, "Do not fear, for am I in the place of God? As for you, you meant evil against me, but *God meant it for good*, to bring it about that many people should be kept alive, as they are today."

The second way the Bible describes the way God fulfilled his prophecy is: The brothers meant the sale of Joseph for evil, but *God meant it for good*. Notice it does not say that God *used* their evil for good after they meant it for evil. It says that in the very act of evil, there were two different designs: In the sinful act, *they* were designing evil, and in the same sinful act, *God* was designing good.

A LIFE-SAVING SIN POINTING TO CHRIST

This is what we have seen and will see over and over: What man designs—or the devil designs—for evil, God designs for some great good. The great good mentioned in Genesis 45:5 is "to preserve life"—the life of the chosen people through whom the Savior of the world will come.

And the great good mentioned in Genesis 50:20 is "to bring it about that many people should be kept alive, as they are today"—the people through whom the Messiah will come. These two descriptions of God's design in this sin are pointers to God's global purpose. Here is a life-saving, people-saving sin. This will prove to be a powerful foreshadowing of the glory of Christ and how the murderous sin against him will also be a saving sin.

Let's look at three things in this story that prepare us to see the glory of Jesus and who he really is.

Salvation Comes through Sin and Suffering

First, we see the general pattern that turns up over and over in the Bible, namely, that God's saving victory for his people often comes through sin and suffering. Joseph's brothers sinned against him, and he suffered for it. And in all this, God is at work to save his people—including the very ones who are trying to destroy the savior. The fact that Jesus came this way should not have been as surprising to as many people as it was. That he was sinned against and suffered on the way to save his people is what we would expect from this pattern that turns up again and again.

So in the story of Joseph and the spectacular sin of his brothers, we are being prepared to see the glory of Christ—his patience and humility and servanthood, all the while saving the very ones who were trying to get rid of him.

> *Died He for me, who caused His pain—*
> *For me, who Him to death pursued?*
> *Amazing love! How can it be*
> *That Thou, my God, shouldst die for me?*[1]

The Suffering One Is Righteous

Second, the story of Joseph and the spectacular sin of his brothers prepares us to see Jesus not just because of the general pattern that God's saving victory for his people often comes through suffering and sin, but more specifically, in this case, because the very one who is suffering and being sinned against is so righteous. Joseph, without being perfect, stands out in this story for his amazing constancy and faithfulness to every relationship.

Even in undeserved exile, he is faithful to Potiphar, and he is faithful to the jailer. Genesis 39:22: "The keeper of the prison

---

[1]Charles Wesley, "And Can It Be That I Should Gain?" (1738).

put Joseph in charge of all the prisoners who were in the prison. Whatever was done there, he was the one who did it."

And what was Joseph's reward? He was lied about by Potiphar's wife, and the cupbearer of Pharaoh, whose dream Joseph interpreted, thanklessly forgot about him in prison for two years after his interpretation.

So the point of all this is not just that there is sin and suffering and that God is at work in it to save his people. More specifically, the point is that the righteous one, even though mistreated for so long, is finally vindicated by God. Even though others have rejected this righteous stone, God makes him the cornerstone (cf. Matt. 21:42). His vindication becomes the very means of the salvation of his persecutors.

Jesus Christ is the final and ultimate and perfect righteous one (Acts 7:52; 1 John 2:1). To others it seemed as if Jesus' life was going so badly that he must be a sinner. But in the end, all the sin against him, and all the suffering he endured in perfect righteousness, led to his vindication and, because of it, to our salvation. If Joseph is amazing in his steadfastness, Jesus is ten thousand times more amazing, because he experienced ten thousand times more suffering, and deserved it ten thousand times less, and was perfectly steadfast, faithful, and righteous through it all.

The Scepter Will Not Depart from Judah

There are other parallels in this story between Joseph and Jesus, but we turn now to the most important thing in this story about Jesus, and it is not a parallel with Joseph. It's a prophecy about the coming of Jesus, which could not have happened if these sinful sons of Jacob had starved in the famine.

The spectacular sin of these brothers was God's way of saving the tribe of Judah from extinction so that the Lion of Judah, Jesus Christ, would be born and die and rise and reign over all the peoples of the world. We see this most clearly in Genesis 49:8–10. Jacob, the father of Joseph, is about to die. Before he dies, he pronounces a prophetic blessing over all his sons. Here is what he says about his son Judah:

> Judah, your brothers shall praise you; your hand shall be on the neck of your enemies; your father's sons shall bow down before you. Judah is a lion's cub; from the prey, my son, you have gone up. He stooped down; he crouched as a lion and as a lioness; who dares rouse him? The scepter shall not depart from Judah, nor the ruler's staff from between his feet, until tribute comes to him; and to him shall be the obedience of the peoples.

Here is a prophecy of the coming final king of Israel, the Lion of Judah, the Messiah. Notice that the scepter—the ruler's staff, the sign of the king—will be in the line of Judah until one comes who is no ordinary king, because *all* the peoples, not just Israel, will obey him. "To him shall be the obedience of the peoples."

This is fulfilled in Jesus. Listen to the way the apostle John describes Jesus' role in heaven after his crucifixion and resurrection:

> "Weep no more; behold, the Lion of the tribe of Judah, the Root of David, has conquered, so that he can open the scroll and its seven seals." . . . And they sang a new song, saying, "Worthy are you to take the scroll and to open its seals, for you were slain, and by your blood you ransomed people for God from every tribe and language and people and nation, and you have made them a kingdom and priests to our God, and they shall reign on the earth." (Rev. 5:5, 9–10)

THE LION OF JUDAH IS THE LAMB WHO WAS SLAIN

The most magnificent thing about the Lion of the tribe of Judah in his fulfillment of Jacob's prophecy is that he lays claim on the obedience of all the peoples of the world not by *exploiting* our guilt and crushing us into submission, but by *bearing* our guilt and freeing us to love him and praise him and obey him with joy forever. The Lion of Judah is the Lamb who was slain. He wins our obedience by forgiving our sins and making his own obedience—his own perfection as the righteous one—the basis of our acceptance with God. And in this position of immeasurable safety and joy—all of it owing to his suffering and righteousness and death and resurrection—he wins our free and happy obedience.

The story of Joseph is the story of a righteous one who is sinned against and suffers so that the tribe of Judah would be preserved and a Lion would come forth and would prove to be a Lamb-like Lion and by his suffering and death purchase and empower glad obedience from all the nations—even from those who put him to death.

Does he have yours?

7

THE SINFUL ORIGIN OF THE SON OF DAVID

How the God-Man Becomes the King of Kings

All the people said to Samuel, "Pray for your servants to the LORD your God, that we may not die, for we have added to all our sins this evil, to ask for ourselves a king." And Samuel said to the people, "Do not be afraid; you have done all this evil. Yet do not turn aside from following the LORD, but serve the LORD with all your heart."

1 SAMUEL 12:19–20

The point of this chapter is that the kingship of Israel—the fact that Israel had kings—was owing in part to sin. It was a spectacular sin for the people of God to say to their Maker and Redeemer, "We want to be like the nations. We do not want you to be our king. We want a human king." That is a spectacular sin. Samuel calls it, in verse 17, a great wickedness. Nevertheless, if Israel had had no kingship, Jesus Christ would not have come as the king of Israel and the Son of David and King of kings. But Christ's kingship over Israel and over the world is not an afterthought in the mind of God. It was not an unplanned response to the sin of Israel. It was part of his plan.

88   S P E C T A C U L A R   S I N S

WHY DO IT THIS WAY?

So our question is: If God saw this spectacular sin coming and he knew that he would permit it and thus make the kingship of Israel part of his plan to glorify Christ as the King of kings, why not just make kingship part of Israel's governance from the beginning? Why not make Moses the first king, then Joshua, and so on? Why plan for a more direct kingship of God himself at the beginning and then bring human kingship into Israel's history later through a spectacular sin?

ABRAHAM AND THE COMING KINGSHIP

Let's begin with the story itself. God chose Abram as the father of the people of Israel in Genesis 12 and promised him that through his offspring all the families of the world will be blessed (Gen. 12:1–3). The Messiah, Jesus Christ, will come through this line.

One of the first things that happens to Abram is that he meets a strange figure named Melchizedek in Genesis 14:18. He is called "priest of God Most High" and "king of Salem." His name means "king of righteousness." The writer of the book of Hebrews, in the New Testament, sees Melchizedek as a type or a prefiguring or foreshadowing of Christ, because Psalm 110:4 says that the coming messianic king is also "a priest forever after the order of Melchizedek." So Hebrews says, "Melchizedek . . . is first, by translation of his name, king of righteousness, and then he is also king of Salem, that is, king of peace . . . resembling the Son of God . . ." (Heb. 7:1–3).

HANNAH AND THE COMING KINGSHIP

So already in the purposes of God, the coming Messiah will be a priest-king. The decision for him to be a king did not come after some other plan failed. We see this again in the story of Samuel's birth and dedication. Recall that his mother Hannah was barren. Then Eli prophesied that she would have a child. Samuel was born, and Hannah brings him to the temple and dedicates him to the Lord.

Among the amazing things that Hannah says, one is found in 1 Samuel 2:10—and remember, this is decades before there was any king in Israel (only when Samuel is an old man do the people press him to give them a king). She says, "The adversaries of the LORD shall be broken to pieces; against them he will thunder in heaven. The LORD will judge the ends of the earth; he will give strength *to his king and exalt the power of his anointed*." In other words, there *will* be a human king in Israel someday.

MOSES AND THE COMING KINGSHIP

Back in Deuteronomy 17:14–20, Moses had given instructions about the kingship for the day that the people would go in that direction. And Deuteronomy 28:36 foretold the exile of the people and their king if they were to rebel against the Lord: "The LORD will bring you *and your king* whom you set over you to a nation that neither you nor your fathers have known."

So I conclude that what happened in 1 Samuel 12 was not a surprise to God. He knew that this spectacular sin would happen, and he knew that he would permit it. And when God intends to permit a thing, he does so wisely, not foolishly. Therefore, this spectacular sin is part of God's overarching plan for the kingship of Israel and for the glory of his Son.

HOW THE KINGSHIP CAME

Let's see how it came about before we ponder why he would do it this way. The demand for a king started back in 1 Samuel 8, but we will pick it up in chapter 12. In verses 8–11, Samuel shows that God himself has been a good king to Israel.

> [The LORD] brought your fathers out of Egypt and made them dwell in this place. But they forgot the LORD their God. And he sold them into the hand of Sisera, commander of the army

of Hazor, and into the hand of the Philistines, and into the hand of the king of Moab. And they fought against them. And they cried out to the LORD and said, "We have sinned, because we have forsaken the LORD and have served the Baals and the Ashtaroth. But now deliver us out of the hand of our enemies, that we may serve you." And the LORD sent Jerubbaal and Barak and Jephthah and Samuel and delivered you out of the hand of your enemies on every side, and you lived in safety.

The point of these verses is to show that God was faithful as their divine king. When they cried to him, he saved them. He gave them safety. That's what a king is for—to provide peace for the people. And what was their response? Verse 12: "And when you saw that Nahash the king of the Ammonites came against you, you said to me [Samuel], 'No, but a king shall reign over us,' when the LORD your God was your king."

You can hear the disbelief in Samuel's voice: You asked for a king when *God* was your king! What should Samuel do? The Lord had already told him in 1 Samuel 8:7–9, "Obey the voice of the people in all that they say to you, for they have not rejected you, but they have rejected me from being king over them. . . . Now then, obey their voice; only you shall solemnly warn them and show them the ways of the king who shall reign over them."

SPECTACULAR SIN: "YOUR WICKEDNESS IS GREAT"

So Samuel says in 1 Samuel 12:13, "Behold, the LORD has set a king over you." Then he calls on the Lord to give them a sign in thunder and rain, and he describes their sin as a great wickedness. Verse 17: "Is it not wheat harvest today? I will call upon the LORD, that he may send thunder and rain. And you shall know and see that *your wickedness is great*, which you have done in the sight of the LORD, in asking for yourselves a king."

And just to make sure we don't miss the holy work of God

through this unholy wickedness, Paul, in Acts 13:20–22, makes explicit that it was *God* who gave Israel her first king. "[God] gave them judges until Samuel the prophet. Then they asked for a king, and *God gave them Saul* the son of Kish, a man of the tribe of Benjamin, for forty years. And when he had removed him, *he raised up David to be their king*." We have seen this repeatedly in the spectacular sins of history. Man meant it for evil, and God meant it for good.

WHAT ARE WE TO LEARN FROM THIS?

So the question is this: If God saw this spectacular sin coming and he knew that he would permit it and thus make the kingship of Israel part of his plan to glorify Christ as the King of kings, why not just make kingship part of Israel's governance from the beginning? Why not make Moses the first king, then Joshua, and so on? Why did God start with himself as the king, and then bring human kingship into Israel's history later through a spectacular sin? What are we to learn from this?

At least six things.

We Are Stiff-Necked, Rebellious, and Unthankful

We should learn from this how stiff-necked and rebellious and unthankful we are. That's why 1 Samuel 12 begins the way it does, reminding the people how God saved them from Egypt and then gave them the Promised Land and then rescued them from evil kings. Each time they forgot God and went after other things.

That is not just the story of Israel. It's the story of humanity. It's the story of my life and your life. Even as Christians, we are not steadfast in our affections for God. We have thankful days and unthankful days. And even our thankful days are not as thankful as they should be. Just think of how joyful and thankful you would be if your heart responded to God himself and his ten thousand gifts with the admiration and gratitude of which he is worthy.

So God gives us pictures of ourselves in stories like this. He allows his people to drift into these kinds of ungrateful and idolatrous seasons so that every mouth may be stopped and the whole world held accountable before God (Rom. 3:19).

God Is Faithful to His Own Name

We should learn from this how faithful God is to his own name. Look at verse 22: "It has pleased the LORD to make you a people *for himself.*" What is the deepest foundation of God's faithfulness? His allegiance to his own name. His passion for his own glory. Read verse 22 slowly and thoughtfully: "The LORD will not forsake his people, *for his great name's sake.*" It does not say for "*their* name's sake" but "for *his* name's sake." God is totally committed to upholding the worth and truth and righteousness of his own name. So stories like this are in the Bible to teach us that God's ways are governed by an infinite wisdom guided by the infinite worth of the name of God.

Grace Flows to Sinners from God's Supreme Allegiance to His Name

We should learn from this how amazingly grace for sinners like us flows from God's supreme allegiance to his own name in the midst of sin. Consider the illustration of this in verses 19–22.

In verse 19, the people are terrified at the spectacular sin they have committed against God. They say, "Pray for your servants to the LORD your God, that we may not die, for we have added to all our sins this evil, to ask for ourselves a king." The words that follow this are a picture of free gospel grace to sinners. Samuel said to the people, "Do not be afraid; you have done all this evil" (v. 20).

Stop right there and be amazed. "Do not be afraid; you have done all this evil." Isn't that a misprint? Shouldn't it say, "*Be afraid*; you have done all this evil"? But it says, "Do *not* be afraid; you have done all this *evil.*" That is pure grace. God's grace treats us not the way we deserve: "Be afraid; you have done all this evil." But better than we deserve: "Do *not* be afraid; you have done all this evil."

How can this be? What is the basis of this grace? Not us! We have done evil. What then? We've seen it already. Verse 22: Don't be afraid, "for the LORD will not forsake his people, for his great name's sake." God's allegiance to his own name is the foundation of his faithfulness to us. If God ever forsook his supreme allegiance to himself, there would be no grace for us. If he based his kindness to us on our worth, there would be no kindness to us.

We are stiff-necked, rebellious, and ungrateful. Free, unmerited grace is our only hope to be otherwise. And the basis of that grace is not the worth of our name, but the infinite worth of God's name. Recall 2 Timothy 2:13: "If we are faithless, he remains faithful—for *he cannot deny himself.*" Allegiance to himself is the ground of his faithfulness to us. God means for us to learn from this spectacular sin that the grace of our salvation is ultimately based not on our value to him, but his value to himself.

Kingship Belongs Only to God

We should learn from God's way of bringing about the kingship in Israel that kingship belongs only to the Lord. God inaugurates his relationship with Israel with no human king in order to make crystal-clear that only God should be the king of Israel. Only God is king. When Israel asked for a king, they were rejecting this truth. God says it plainly in 1 Samuel 8:7: "They have rejected me from being king over them." If God had begun the history of Israel with Moses and Joshua being the first kings, it would not be clear that only God can be the rightful king of Israel. He will have no merely human competitors.

A God-Man Must Be King

Therefore, we should learn from God's way of installing a human king what his purposes are. He meant to inaugurate a line of human kings who would all fail until the King came who was not only man but also God. This follows from the double fact that, on the one hand, all ordinary humans fail and, on the other hand, only God can be king of Israel in the fullest sense. In giving Israel a human king, God did not change his mind about only God being the full and rightful king of Israel. The point is that God alone is King of Israel, and there is coming a King, a Son of David, who will not fail like the others. He will not be just another sinful man. He will be the God-man.

The last question on the lips of Jesus that silences the Pharisees is based on Psalm 110:1, where David says, "The LORD [God] says to my Lord [the coming king and Messiah]: 'Sit at my right hand, until I make your enemies your footstool.'" Jesus quotes this and then asks his adversaries, "If then David calls him [the Messiah] Lord, how is he his [David's] son?" (Matt. 22:45).

In other words, for those who have ears to hear, Jesus is *more* than the son of David. He is more than a merely human king. "In the beginning was the Word, and the Word was with God, and the Word *was God*. . . . And the Word became flesh and dwelt among us, and we have seen his glory, glory as of the only Son from the Father" (John 1:1, 14). Only God can be the final rightful king of Israel. That's the way it began. That is the way it ends. Jesus Christ is the divine-human king of Israel.

The King Died for His People

Finally, we should learn from the way God brought a human king to Israel that there needed to be a *human* king. Only God can be the rightful king of Israel. But there needed to be a human king. Why? Because for God to have a people to rule and to love, who were not in hell because of their sins, the king had to die for the people. And God can't die. Man can die. So God had planned not only that God himself was the full and rightful king of Israel, but also that the rightful king of Israel must die in the place of the people. So the king of Israel is the *God*-man so that the king can be God, but he is also the God-*man* so that the king can die.

When Samuel said, "Do not be afraid, you rebellious, stiff-necked, ungrateful sinners; you have done all this evil" (1 Sam. 12:20), what was the basis of this grace? It was the value of God's name. "The LORD will not forsake his people, for his great name's sake" (v. 22). The upholding and the vindication of God's name is the basis of grace.

And where was that vindication most decisively and finally displayed? Answer: in the cross of Christ. Romans 3:25: "God put [Christ] forward as a propitiation by his blood, to be received by faith. This was to show God's righteousness, because in his divine forbearance he had passed over former sins."

AT THE CROSS, FOR HIS NAME'S SAKE

Indeed, he had passed over sins. On this very day when the people deserved to be destroyed for asking for a king, God forgave them and passed over their sins—for his name's sake. But God can't sweep sin under the rug of the universe and still uphold his name as a righteous and holy God. Sin must be dealt with. It must be punished. And it was, when Jesus died.

The only reason that sinful people like us can have a king as great and glorious and powerful and good and holy and wise as Jesus, without being consumed for our sin, is that God planned for the king to die for his subjects and rise again. In every Gospel, Jesus is asked just before he dies, "Are you the king of the Jews?" And he answers, "You have said so" (Matt. 27:11; Mark 15:2; Luke 23:3; John 18:33).

THE COMING KING OF ALL

And not just the king of the Jews, but the king of all—especially those who trust him. He is seated at the right hand of the Father today until all his enemies are put under his feet and all his elect are gathered in from all the peoples of the earth. Then the end will come. And Christ "will appear a second time, not to deal with sin but to save those who are eagerly waiting for him" (Heb. 9:28). And "on his robe and on his thigh he has a name written"—not king of the Jews, but "King of kings and Lord of lords" (Rev. 19:16). Amen. Come, King Jesus.

8

JUDAS ISCARIOT, THE SUICIDE OF SATAN, AND THE SALVATION OF THE WORLD

How God Conquered Sin through Sin

Then Satan entered into Judas called Iscariot, who was of the number of the twelve. He went away and conferred with the chief priests and officers how he might betray him to them. And they were glad, and agreed to give him money. So he consented and sought an opportunity to betray him to them in the absence of a crowd.

LUKE 22:3–6

The aim of this book has been to show that over and over in the history of the world, the epoch-making sins that changed the course of history never nullified but only fulfilled the global purposes of God to glorify his Son and save his people.

My prayer is that as these great historical vistas of God's sovereignty over sin take their place in your mind, they would have a profoundly practical effect in making you strong in the face of breath-stopping sorrows and making you bold for Christ in the face of dangerous opposition—Christ-exalting strength in calamity and Christ-exalting courage in conflict. I pray that the Lord will weave cords of steel and silk into the fabric of your soul.

HISTORY'S MOST SPECTACULAR SIN: THE MURDER OF JESUS

The most spectacular sin that has ever been committed in the history of the world is the brutal murder of Jesus Christ, the morally perfect, infinitely worthy, divine Son of God. And probably the most despicable act in the process of this murder was the betrayal of Jesus by one of his closest friends, Judas Iscariot.

Judas was one of the twelve apostles whom Jesus had personally chosen and who had been with Jesus during his entire public ministry. He had been entrusted with the moneybag for the whole group (John 13:29). He was close enough to Jesus at the Last Supper to be dipping bread with him in the same cup (Mark 14:20).

"SATAN ENTERED INTO JUDAS"

On the night of the Last Supper, Luke tells us in Luke 22:3–6 that "Satan entered into Judas. . . . He went away and conferred with the chief priests and officers how he might betray [Jesus] to them. And they were glad, and agreed to give him money. So he consented and sought an opportunity to betray him to them in the absence of a crowd." Later he led the authorities to Jesus in the Garden of Gethsemane and betrayed Jesus with a kiss (Luke 22:47–48). With that, Jesus' death was sealed.

When Luke tells us in verse 3 that "Satan entered into Judas," several questions come to our minds. One is whether Satan simply mastered a good Judas or whether Judas was already walking sinfully in step with Satan, and Satan simply decided that now was the time. Another question is why Satan would do this, since the death and resurrection of Jesus would result in Satan's final defeat, and there is good reason to think that Satan knew that. And the third and most important question is: Where was God when this happened? What was his role or non-role in the most spectacular sin that ever was? Let's take these questions one at a time.

SATAN'S POWER IN JUDAS' SINFUL PASSIONS

When it says in Luke 22:3 that "Satan entered into Judas," how are we to think about the will of Judas and the power of Satan? Judas was not an innocent bystander when Satan entered into him. The apostle John tells us in John 12:6 that he was a "thief." When Judas complained that Mary had wasted money in anointing Jesus, John comments, "He said this, not because he cared about the poor, but because he was a thief, and having charge of the moneybag he used to help himself to what was put into it."

If that sounds incredible, just think of the scandalous behavior of so-called Christian leaders today who use ministry gifts to buy $40,000 worth of clothes at one store in a year, and send their kids on a $30,000 trip to the Bahamas, and drive a white Lexus and a red Mercedes. As Judas sat beside Jesus with his pious, religious face and went out and cast out demons in Jesus' name, he was not a righteous lover of Jesus. He loved money. He loved the power and pleasures that money could buy.

Paul tells us how that works together with Satan's power. Listen to Ephesians 2:1–3: "You were dead in the trespasses and sins in which you once walked, following the course of this world, following the prince of the power of the air [*notice the connection: dead in sins, following Satan*], the spirit that is now at work in the sons of disobedience—among whom we all once lived in the passions of our flesh, carrying out the desires of the body and the mind, and were by nature children of wrath, like the rest of mankind." Dead in our sins, walking in the passions of the flesh, fulfilling the desires of body and mind, and *therefore* following the prince of the power of the air.

Satan does not take innocent people captive. There are no

innocent people. Satan has power where sinful passions hold sway. Judas was a lover of money, and he covered it with a phony, external relationship with Jesus. And then he sold him for thirty pieces of silver. How many of his ilk are still around today! Don't be one. And don't be duped by one.

SATAN'S ROLE IN HIS OWN DESTRUCTION

The second question is why Satan would lead Judas to betray Jesus. Didn't he know that the death and resurrection of Jesus would result in his final defeat (Col. 2:13–15; Rev. 12:11)? There is good reason to think Satan knew that.

When Jesus began his ministry on the way to the cross, Satan tried to turn him away from the path of suffering and sacrifice. In the wilderness, he tempted him to turn stones into bread and jump off the temple and get the rulership of the world by worshiping him (Matt. 4:1–11). The point of all these temptations is: "Don't walk the path of suffering and sacrifice and death. Use your power to escape suffering. If you're the Son of God, show your right to reign. And I can help you do it. Whatever you do, don't go to the cross."

And remember the time when Jesus predicted he would suffer many things from the elders and the chief priests and be killed, and Peter rebuked him and said, "Far be it from you, Lord! This shall never happen to you" (Matt. 16:22). In other words, I will never let you be killed like that.

Jesus did not commend Peter. He said, "Get behind me, Satan! You are a hindrance to me. For you are not setting your mind on the things of God, but on the things of man" (Matt. 16:23). Hindering Jesus from going to the cross was the work of Satan. Satan did not want Jesus crucified. It would be his undoing.

But here he is in Luke 22:3 entering into Judas and leading him to betray the Lord and bring him to the cross. Why the about-face? Why try to divert him from the cross and then take the initiative to bring him to the cross? We are not told. Here is my effort at an answer.

Satan saw that his efforts to divert Jesus from the cross had failed. Time after time Jesus kept the course. His face was set like flint to die (Luke 9:51, 53), and Satan concluded that there was no stopping him. Therefore, he resolved that if he couldn't stop it, he would at least make it as ugly and painful and as heartbreaking as possible. Not just death, but death by betrayal. Death by abandonment. Death by denial (Luke 22:31–34). Death by torture. If he could not stop it, he would drag others into it and do as much damage as he could. It was a spectacular sequence of sins that brought Jesus to the cross.

GOD'S ROLE IN THE MURDER OF HIS SON

Which brings us now to the third and final question—the most important one: Where was God when this happened? Or more precisely: What was God's role or non-role in the most spectacular sin that ever happened—the murder of Jesus Christ?

To answer a question like that we should put our hands on our mouths and silence our philosophical speculations. Our opinions don't count here. All that counts is what God himself has shown us in his word. And the first thing he shows us is that the details surrounding the death of Jesus were prophesied in God's word hundreds of years before they happened.

The Scriptures show that evil men would reject Jesus when he came. "Jesus said to them [quoting Psalm 118:22], 'Have you never read in the Scriptures: "The stone that the builders rejected has become the cornerstone; this was the Lord's doing, and it is marvelous in our eyes"?'" (Matt. 21:42).

The Scriptures showed that Jesus must be hated. Jesus quoted Psalm 35:19 and said, "The word that is written in their Law must be fulfilled: 'They hated me without a cause'" (John 15:25).

The Scriptures showed that the disciples would abandon Jesus. Jesus quotes Zechariah 13:7: "You will all fall away because of me this night. For it is written, 'I will strike the shepherd, and the sheep of the flock will be scattered'" (Matt. 26:31).

The Scriptures showed that Jesus would be pierced, but none of his bones would be broken. John quotes Psalm 34:20 and Zechariah 12:10 and says, "One of the soldiers pierced his side with a spear. . . . For these things took place that the Scripture might be fulfilled: 'Not one of his bones will be broken.' And again another Scripture says, 'They will look on him whom they have pierced'" (John 19:34–37).

The Scriptures showed that Jesus would be betrayed by a close friend for thirty pieces of silver. Jesus cites Psalm 41:9 and says, "I am not speaking of all of you; I know whom I have chosen. But the Scripture will be fulfilled, 'He who ate my bread has lifted his heel against me'" (John 13:18). In Matthew 26:24, Jesus says, "The Son of Man goes as it is written of him, but woe to that man by whom the Son of Man is betrayed!" And Matthew 27:9–10 says, "Then was fulfilled what had been spoken by the prophet Jeremiah, saying, 'And they took the thirty pieces of silver, the price of him on whom a price had been set by some of the sons of Israel, and they gave them for the potter's field, as the Lord directed me'" (Jer. 19:1–13; Zech. 11:12–13).

And not only the Scriptures, but Jesus himself declared, down to the details, how he would be killed. In Mark 10:33–34 he says, "See, we are going up to Jerusalem, and the Son of Man will be delivered over to the chief priests and the scribes, and they will condemn him to death and deliver him over to the Gentiles. And they will mock him and spit on him, and flog him and kill him. And after three days he will rise." And on that last night, Jesus looked at Peter and said, "Truly, I tell you, this very night, before the rooster crows, you will deny me three times" (Matt. 26:34).

ACCORDING TO HIS SOVEREIGN WILL

From all these prophecies, we know that God foresaw and did not prevent and therefore included in his plan that his Son would be rejected, hated, abandoned, betrayed, denied, condemned, spit upon, flogged, mocked, pierced, and killed. All these were explicitly in God's mind before they actually happened as things that he planned would happen to Jesus. These things did not just happen. They were foretold in God's word. God knew they would happen and could have planned to stop them, but didn't. So they happened according to his sovereign will. His plan.

And all of them were evil. They were sin. It is surpassingly sinful to reject, hate, abandon, betray, deny, condemn, spit upon, flog, mock, pierce, and kill the morally perfect, infinitely worthy, divine Son of God. And yet the Bible is explicit and clear that God himself planned these things. This is explicit not only in all the prophetic texts we have seen, but also in passages that say even more plainly that God ordained that these things come to pass.

GOD BROUGHT IT TO PASS

For example, Isaiah 53:6, 10 says, "All we like sheep have gone astray; we have turned every one to his own way; and *the LORD has laid on him the iniquity of us all. . . . It was the will of the LORD to crush him*; he has put him to grief." The Lord crushed him. God was at work in all the circumstances that brought Jesus to the cross. Behind the spitting and flogging and mocking and piercing is the invisible hand and plan of God.

And I say that carefully and with trembling. This truth is too big and too weighty and too shocking to be glib about or to be cocky about. I choose to say that *the invisible hand and plan of God* are behind these most spectacular sins in all the universe—more grievous and more spectacular than the Fall of Satan or any other sins. The reason I use these very words is because the Bible says it in these very words.

THE HAND AND PLAN OF GOD

In Acts 4:27–28 we have the clearest, most explicit statement about God's hand and plan behind the horrific crucifixion of his Son. "Truly in this city there were gathered together against your holy servant Jesus, whom you anointed, both Herod and Pontius Pilate, along with the Gentiles and the peoples of Israel, to do whatever your *hand* and your *plan* had predestined to take place." Those are the two words I am using: the *hand* of God and the *plan* of God.

It is a strange way of speaking—to say that God's *hand* and *plan* have predestined something to happen. One does not ordinarily think of God's "hand" predestining. How does a hand predestine? Here's what I think it means: The hand of God ordinarily stands for God's exerted power—not power in the abstract, but earthly, effective exertions of power. The point of combining it with "plan" is to say that it is not just a theoretical plan; it is a plan that will be executed by God's own hand.

This explains Isaiah 53:10: "It was the will of the LORD to bruise him; he has put him to grief." Or more literally, with the King James Version, "It pleased the LORD to bruise him; he hath put him to grief." The Lord bruised him. Behind Herod and Pilate and the Gentiles and the people of Israel was Jesus' own Father who loved him with an infinite love.

THE GOSPEL: GOD AT WORK IN DEATH

Why should this matter to you? It should matter because if God were not the main Actor in the death of Christ, then the death of Christ could not save us from our sins, and we would perish in hell forever (Matt. 25:46; 2 Thess. 1:9). The reason the death of Christ is the heart of the gospel—the heart of the good news—is that God was doing it. Romans 5:8: "*God* shows his love for us in that while we were still sinners, Christ died for us." If you separate God's activity from the death of Jesus, you lose the gospel. This was God's doing. It is the highest and deepest point of his love for sinners. His love for you.

Romans 8:3: "*Sending his own Son* in the likeness of sinful flesh and for sin, he condemned sin in the flesh." God condemned sin in Jesus' flesh with our condemnation. So we are free.

Galatians 3:13: "Christ redeemed us from the curse of the law by becoming a curse for us." *God cursed Jesus* with the curse that belonged on us. So we are free.

2 Corinthians 5:21: "For our sake he [*God*] made him to be sin who knew no sin, so that in him we might become the righteousness of God." God imputed our sin to him, and now we go free in God's righteousness.

Isaiah 53:5: "He was wounded for our transgressions; he was crushed for our iniquities." *God wounded him.* God crushed him. For you and me. And we go free.

THE CROSS OF CHRIST: THE WORK AND LOVE OF GOD

The reason why this book matters is this. If you embrace the biblical truth (and I pray you will) that God ordains spectacular sins for the global glory of his Son, without God in any way becoming unholy or unrighteous or sinful in that act, then you will not shrink back from the cross of Christ as a work of God. You will not be among the number of those who call the world's most loving act "divine child abuse." You will come to the cross and fall on your face. And you will say: This is no mere human conspiracy. This is the work of God and the love of God. You will receive it as his highest gift. And you will be saved. And Christ will be glorified. And I will not have written in vain.

A CLOSING
PRAYER

My aim has been to strengthen your faith in the goodness and mercy and wisdom and power of God, not just in the midst of calamity, but in the very sins that are woven into the calamity. When you are tempted to forsake God because of the greatness of evil and misery in the world, may you remember that the Bible has prepared us for this temptation. It has shown us over and over that sin and sickness and disaster never escape the good governance of the infinitely wise God. Whether it is Satan or Adam or Joseph or Judas, the great divine dictum holds: "You meant evil against me, but God meant it for good" (Gen. 50:20).

The most spectacular sins are not signs of ultimate absurdity. Satan is the ultimately irrational being. And much of what he is allowed to do will have the mark of senselessness on it. That is why there is truth in a president's words when he gives his news conference after a calamity and describes a mass murder as "senseless killing." But there is another vantage point. Namely, God's: Yes, senseless at one level, but not ultimately.

Far, far above thy thought,
His counsel shall appear,
When fully He the work hath wrought,
That caused thy needless fear.[1]

The Bible does not say that perseverance in faith through the horrors of sin and misery will be easy. That is why it says, "The one

---

[1]Paul Gerhardt, "Give to the Winds Thy Fears," 1656 (translated 1737 by John Wesley).

who *conquers*" will not be hurt by the second death. The first death, yes, and it may be horrible. But not the second (Rev. 2:10–11). Maintaining the joy of faith in the face of horrific evil does not happen by coasting. It happens by conquering. That is my aim. That you would conquer unbelief and despair in the face of spectacular sin and misery. To that end, I would like to pray for you.

> *Gracious and glorious Father,*
> *because you are rich in mercy,*
> *and great in love,*
> *and sovereign in grace,*
> *we ask that you would make this little book*
> *a window onto the panorama of your glory,*
> *and a skylight to your supremacy in all things.*
>
> *By the truth-loving power of your Holy Spirit*
> *grant that the glass pane would be clean—*
> *that what is faithful to your word would be confirmed,*
> *and what is not would be forgiven, not confusing.*
> *We ask that your cloud-banishing illumination*
> *would be given to our minds,*
> *and that spiritual understanding would fill our hearts,*
> *and that according to the command of your apostle,*
> *we would grow in the grace and knowledge*
> *of our Lord and Savior Jesus Christ.*
>
> *May we see the spectacular sins of the world*
> *as horrible as they are.*
> *And may we see the holiness of God*
> *as pure as it is.*
> *And may we see the rule of God over the sin of man*
> *as righteous as it is.*
> *And thus grant the steel of ultimate reality*
> *to strengthen the spine of our faith,*
> *and sweeten our lips for the bruised heart.*

Put the ballast of biblical truth
in the belly of our little boats,
lest the crashing waves of calamity
in these changing times
cause us to capsize in the sea of trouble.

And according to your apostle's warning,
forbid that the increase of our knowledge
would cause the increase of our pride.
Rather, O God of infinite wisdom,
reveal, with all our understanding,
the unfathomable sinfulness of our hearts without Christ,
and the infinitesimal smallness of our strength
in comparison to yours,
and the absolute dependence of our life on you,
and the unfathomable depths of your judgments,
and how dim is the mirror in which we see.

Grant to our minds and hearts
new and deeper capacities to see and savor
the glories of Jesus Christ.
With every new glimpse of his glory in your word,
let there awaken new affections in our hearts.
Ignite our souls to treasure Christ in a way that
destroys our sinful lusts
and delights the deepest recesses of our being
and displays his truth and beauty
to a world that does not know
that this is what it needs more than anything.
And from this all-satisfying treasuring of Christ
may there flow a liberation from selfishness,
and a triumph over bitterness and anger,
and a freedom from worry and fear,
and victory over depression and discouragement,
and the severing of every root of sensual lust.

All this freedom, Lord, we seek for the sake of love.
Grant that our contentment in Christ would be a
dissatisfied contentment,
eager to expand by including others.
Grant that the joy of the Lord would not be a solitary joy,
but the strength to sacrifice
for the good of others,
even those who hate us.
May brokenhearted boldness
and contrite courage
attend all our deeds of compassion
and all our commendations of Christ to a lost world.
Awaken in us tender affections
for those who hurt,
and self-forgetful attentiveness
for those in our presence.

And in this treasuring of Christ for his supreme glory
and this overflowing love for others,
may Jesus be exalted above all things—
honored, admired, adored, esteemed, enjoyed,
praised, extolled, thanked, and worshiped.
May our light shine in this world
so that people see you in our sacrificial deeds of love
and our uncompromising words of truth
and give glory to your hallowed name,
Father.

Through Jesus Christ,
your Son,
Amen.

ACKNOWLEDGMENTS

I have a Great Shepherd whom God raised from the dead so that through him everything I need in order to do his will would be given (Heb. 13:20–21). And so it has. If I stumble, there is no blaming the lack of my Shepherd's sufficiency or provision. My stumbling is my sin, not his. He always does what is right. And if I stand, it is owing to his power. I get the Shepherd-care. He gets the Shepherd-glory. So my first acknowledgment is that everything good and true is owing to the grace of my Shepherd, Jesus Christ.

Under this Great Shepherd, I am a non-great shepherd of Bethlehem Baptist Church. I thank them for being the kind of flock who draws out of me joyful efforts of exposition. They are a hungry and holy band of disciples. I love speaking of Christ to those who love him so much. This book was first my word to them. And they graciously let me take the time to put those messages into the form of this book.

David Mathis and Nathan Miller stand by me to serve in every way that helps me do this work of shepherding and writing. Carol Steinbach is a faithful friend and partner at Desiring God who indexes my books with excellence to the glory of God. I do not take for granted such a boon of ready and gifted assistance. I thank God for it and pray that I will be a good steward of it.

Noël, as always, blessed me as I disappeared to a borrowed cabin in Wisconsin to transform sermons into chapters. She bears graciously the burden of being married to an imperfect shepherd-author.

The Crossway Books team shares my mission to spread a

passion for the supremacy of God in all things for the joy of all peoples through Jesus Christ. That is why I love working with them.

May the influences and labors of so many not be in vain, as the purpose of things reaches its climax in the glory of Jesus Christ.

SCRIPTURE
INDEX

GENERAL
INDEX

⁂ desiringGod

If you would like to further explore the vision of God and life presented in this book, we at Desiring God would love to serve you. We have hundreds of resources to help you grow in your passion for Jesus Christ and help you spread that passion to others. At our website, desiringGod.org, you'll find almost everything John Piper has written and preached, including more than thirty books. We've made over twenty-five years of his sermons available free online for you to read, listen to, download, and in some cases watch.

In addition, you can access hundreds of articles, listen to our daily internet radio program, find out where John Piper is speaking, learn about our conferences, discover our God-centered children's curricula, and browse our online store. John Piper receives no royalties from the books he writes and no compensation from Desiring God. The funds are all reinvested into our gospel-spreading efforts. DG also has a whatever-you-can-afford policy, designed for individuals with limited discretionary funds. If you'd like more information about this policy, please contact us at the address or phone number below. We exist to help you treasure Jesus Christ and his gospel above all things because he is most glorified in you when you are most satisfied in him. Let us know how we can serve you!

Desiring God
Post Office Box 2901
Minneapolis, Minnesota 55402

888.346.4700
mail@desiringGod.org
www.desiringGod.org